Aug 2018

Mandela Time Line

1912: African National Congress (ANC) established

1918: Mandela born 18 July, Mvuso, Transkei

1927: Father dies, brought up by Thembu Regent.
1939: Enrols at Fort Hare College.

1940: Expelled from Fort Hare.

1941: Moves to Johannesburg, meets Walter Sisulu.

1942: Obtains BA degree and enrols at Witwatersrand University in Faculty of Law.

1944: Joins ANC. Marries Sisulu's cousin, Evelyn. Helps found ANC Youth League.

1945: First child, a son, Thembi born, family allocated a house in Orlando East, Soweto.

1947: Elected Secretary of ANC Youth League.

1948: Afrikaner National Party wins General Election and begins to implement apartheid.

1950: Suppression of Communism Act introduced. Second son, Makgatho, born.

1951: Youth League and Indian Congress organise national work stoppage 26 June. Mandela elected Youth League President.

1952: Defiance of Unjust Laws Campaign 26 June, Mandela and others arrested. Elected President Transvaal ANC, and with Sisulu and others charged and sentenced to nine months hard labour suspended for two years. Banned for attending meetings or gatherings for six months.

1953: His ban expires, but is banned for further two years. Sets up a legal practice with Oliver Tambo.

1954: The Congress Alliance established and daughter Makaziwe is born.

1955: Congress of the People convened to adopt the Freedom Charter. Mandela's ban expires.

1956: Mandela separates from Evelyn. Banned for five years. With 155 others charged with treason.

1957: Mandela meets Winnie Madikizela.

1958: Congress Alliance calls for a national stay-away. Africanist dissidents in ANC split away to form the Pan-Africanist Congress under Robert Sobukwe. Divorces Evelyn. Marries Winnie.

1959: ANC and PAC organise separate anti-pass law campaigns. Daughter Zeni born.

1960: 21 March Sharpeville: police shoot 69 dead and wound 180. State of Emergency declared. Mandela, Sisulu and thousands of others arrested. Tambo sent overseas to represent ANC. Daughter Zindzi born.

1961: South Africa becomes Republic of South Africa—expelled from Commonwealth. Mandela's ban expires. He and all other Treason Trial accused acquitted. Mandela and other ANC members set up *Umkhonto we Sizwe* ('Spear of the Nation, or MK'). 12-day detention without trial introduced.

1962: Goes underground and leaves country. Returns home, arrested 5 August in Natal. October brought to trial in Pretoria, sentenced to five years imprisonment on Robben Island.

1963: May 90-Day Detention without trial introduced. October, Rivonia Trial begins.

1964: Rivonia Trial. Mandela and most others accused found guilty of sabotage, sentenced to life imprisonment on Robben Island.

1965: John Harris only white man in resistance hanged. Other ARM members sentenced 5–15 years.

1967: ANC President Chief Albert Luthuli killed by passing train.

1968: Mandela's mother dies, refused permission to attend funeral.

1969: Winnie and 21 others detained in Pretoria for six months. Then released, Winnie served with a further banning order and house arrested.

1970: Allowed first visit from Winnie in two years.

1973: Refuses state offer of release to the Transkei.

1974: Winnie begins six month jail sentence for communicating with more than one other person.

1975: Winnie's banning order expires, visits Mandela on Robben Island.

1976: Soweto erupts.

1977: Steve Biko killed by police while under arrest. Winnie banned and banished to remote Brandfort.

1978: Winnie sentenced to six months imprisonment suspended for four years.

1980: Release Mandela Campaign begins.

1982: Mandela and several others moved to Pollsmoor Prison near Cape Town.

1983: United Democratic Front (UDF) launched.

1984: Worldwide demands made for Mandela's release. Elections for the first three-chamber South African Parliament: Whites, Coloureds and Indians.

1985: President offers Mandela and other Rivonia Trialists a conditional release. All refuse.

1986: Winnie's house in Brandfort petrol bombed and burned down. She returns to her Soweto home.

1988: Mandela's 70th birthday celebrated worldwide. Admitted to hospital in Cape Town, recovers and in December moved to cottage at Victor Verster Prison outside Cape Town.

1989: July meets President Botha. October all other Rivonia trialists released. December meets F.W. de Klerk, the new President.

1990: Released 11 February. ANC suspends armed struggle.

1992: March, whites-only Referendum approves freedom negotiations by two-thirds majority. April, Mandela and Winnie separate.

1993: Transitional Executive Council set up to work with government to prepare for General Election in 1994. Mandela asks UN to end its economic sanctions. Mandela and de Klerk joint winners of Nobel Peace Prize.

1994: General Election 27 April, ANC elected by a landslide. Inaugurated as President 10 May, with Thabo Mbeki and F.W. de Klerk Deputy Presidents.

1995: Salutes South African Springboks winning Rugby World Cup final Johannesburg.

1996: Truth and Reconciliation Commission (TRC) launched. National Party withdraws from Government of National Unity. New Constitution ratified by Parliament. Divorces Winnie.

1998: Marries Graça Machel. TRC report completed.

1999: Makes farewell speech to Parliament. General Election, Mbeki becomes President.

2003: Hosts 46664 concert on AIDs awareness.

2004: Announces 'retiring from retirement'.

2007: Speaks as his statute unveiled in Parliament Square, London.

2008: July, speaks at 90th birthday concert in London's Hyde Park.

2009: attends ANC pre-election rally, Johannesburg. Greeted ecstatically but too frail to speak. Gives video message at FIFA World Cup Draw.

2010: 20th anniversary of release from prison: attends opening of South Africa's parliament. Attends FIFA World Cup Final Johannesburg.

2013 Dies 5 December, Houghton Johannesburg.

Mandela

What counts in life is not the mere fact
that we have lived.
It is what difference we have made
to the lives of others.

Mandela

His Essential Life

Peter Hain

ROWMAN &
LITTLEFIELD
—————— INTERNATIONAL ——————

London • New York

Published by Rowman & Littlefield International, Ltd.
Unit A, Whitacre Mews, 26–34 Stannary Street, London SE11 4AB
www.rowmaninternational.com

Rowman & Littlefield International, Ltd., is an affiliate of
Rowman & Littlefield
4501 Forbes Boulevard, Suite 200, Lanham, Maryland 20706, USA
With additional offices in Boulder, New York, Toronto (Canada), and
Plymouth (UK)
www.rowman.com

Distributed by NATIONAL BOOK NETWORK

British Library Cataloguing in Publication Data

A catalogue record for this book is available from the British Library

ISBN: HB 978-1-78660-757-7
      PB 978-1-78660-758-4

Library of Congress Cataloging-in-Publication Data

Names: Hain, Peter, 1950- author.
Title: Mandela : his essential life / Peter Hain.
Description: Lanham, Maryland : Rowman & Littlefield, 2018. | Includes
    bibliographical references and index.
Identifiers: LCCN 2018001450 (print) | LCCN 2018001901 (ebook) | ISBN
    978-1-78660-759-1 (Electronic) | ISBN 978-1-78660-757-7 (cloth : alk.
    paper) | ISBN 978-1-78660-758-4 (pbk. : alk. paper)
Subjects: LCSH: Mandela, Nelson, 1918–2013. | Presidents—South
    Africa—Biography. | Political prisoners—South Africa—Biography. |
    Apartheid. | Anti-apartheid movements—South Africa. | African National
    Congress. | South Africa—Politics and government—20th century.
Classification: LCC DT1974 (ebook) | LCC DT1974 .H35 2018 (print) |
    DDC 968.065092—dc23
LC record available at https://lccn.loc.gov/2018001450

♾ ™ The paper used in this publication meets the minimum requirements of
American National Standard for Information Sciences—Permanence of Paper
for Printed Library Materials, ANSI/NISO Z39.48–1992.

Printed in the United States of America

For Adelaine and Walter Hain, among many thousands also heroes in the freedom struggle.

Mandela became the icon, the moral giant so revered by the world, because he had demonstrated that former enemies could become friends.
—ARCHBISHOP DESMOND TUTU

Contents

Preface

A great deal has been written about Nelson Mandela's life, including several excellent, though learned and very lengthy, books that I have drawn upon.

What's been missing, though, is a short, popular and accessible book that tells Mandela's entire and remarkable story in a nutshell—which is what this aims to do. I was not an impartial observer in his life but rather an active participant: initially as an anti-apartheid activist and then as a British politician and friend.

I am especially grateful to my late father, Walter Hain, for his help with research, and to my mother Adelaine Hain—both have always been an inspiration to me, to their large family and to many others—for their courage in the anti-apartheid struggle and their fundamental and selfless decency.

Much thanks also to Elizabeth Haywood, my wife, who gave me great support in the writing and commented invaluably on the draft; to John Battersby, Richard Calland, Fiona Lloyd and Andre Odendaal for their insight and help; and especially to Verne Sheldon Harris of the Nelson Mandela Foundation.

Peter Hain
Ynysygerwn, Neath
February 2018

International Icon

Johannesburg, April 26, 1994. Nelson Mandela and author Peter Hain after the ANC eve-of-election press conference. George Hallett

It was a beautiful, clear autumn day as Nelson Mandela paused and looked up. Stretched out in front of him was Pretoria, the old capital of the system of racial tyranny in South Africa known as 'apartheid' (meaning 'separateness'). Below, the vast nonracial crowd hushed, waiting expectantly. Many could hardly credit they were actually witnessing his installation as the new president of South Africa.

Was this for real? Was the man who had been locked up for

ten thousand days in the prime of his life, most of it on Robben Island off Cape Town's coast, and was the longtime hated 'terrorist' of white folklore now about to assume the highest office in the land as a revered figure after a magnificent election victory? Would they wake up and find it was all a dream?

Hours before, tens of thousands of blacks had poured onto the carefully manicured green lawns stretching below the Union Buildings, the fine old colonial seat of government. They had done so with some trepidation. Not simply because they feared Mandela's induction might be snatched away at the last moment. Not simply because they were still in a state of suspended disbelief at the democratic transformation of the country. But because in the old days, blacks—except for nannies in charge of white children—were not even allowed to step onto the grass they now carpeted so joyously; like many of the country's fine parks, it had always been reserved for whites. (I remember playing there as a boy in the 1960s.)

The symbols of change were everywhere. On top of one of the much-feared Casspirs—the military vehicles that had terrorized the black townships ringing white suburbs—stood the new national flag, which fluttered languidly in the sunshine. Overhead a flock of jets—some in past years used in combat against Mandela's African National Congress (ANC)—screamed over to salute the new president. Alongside the crowd, police officers and soldiers relaxed when only a few years before they would have harassed and intimidated.

No, the people didn't have to pinch themselves, nor did the hundreds of millions across the world who watched live coverage on television. It was no mirage. Today was May 10, 1994. The ANC had been elected by a landslide, and Nelson Mandela was about to take the oath of office. For the first time in modern history, a highly privileged elite—perhaps the most privileged of all in modern times—had given up power voluntarily. This was not after a violent putsch but, even if reluctantly, in a relatively peaceful and democratic way. The people were correct: it was indeed a miracle.

This is a story of that miracle, or more especially of the international icon who weaved his magic to help make it possible. Millions worldwide took part in the long and bitter, but ultimately victorious, anti-apartheid struggle. Most were foot soldiers in the rise and fall of apartheid, including my family and me. Some played an absolutely decisive role; many, a significant one. Nelson Mandela was the leader: in the resistance, in prison, after his release in February 1990 and finally, when in power.

—

Having previously been jailed, silenced by being declared banned persons and deprived of earning a living, my white, South African–born parents and their four children sailed out of Cape Town in 1966, past Robben Island and into exile in Britain.

I was then aged sixteen and remember looking out, feeling queasy as the ocean liner heaved heavily in the Cape rollers and imagining how Nelson Mandela was surviving in his cold, bleak cell where he was then into the third of his long twenty-seven years in prison.

As an African he was permitted no more than five ounces of meat daily where Coloureds (mixed race) were allowed six ounces. He was permitted half an ounce of fat daily; Coloureds, a full ounce. The pernicious precision of apartheid penetrated every nook and cranny of life, banning interracial sex, park benches, sport, jobs, schools, hospitals and so on.

The white-minority-controlled police state had hoped that, out of sight, he would be out of mind on this former leper colony of Robben Island with its freezing cold waters that for generations had devoured all escapees.

But the longer he was imprisoned, the bigger his global profile became. By July 1988, his seventieth birthday became a global celebration with a pulsating 'Free Mandela' rock concert studded with stars at London's Wembley Stadium, attended by one hundred thousand and watched on live television by six hundred million worldwide.

And then, almost miraculously, came something anti-apartheid campaigners had dreamed of—but deep down doubted would ever happen. In February 1990, Nelson Mandela walked out of prison to freedom, an image forever imprinted on me and on many millions—perhaps even billions—who watched it happen on television across the world, many tearful with joy and emotion.

'Almost miraculously' because history gets compressed and rewritten over time, and we tend to take change for granted. But the reality was very different. Nelson Mandela's struggle for freedom—and that of his African National Congress—was long and bitter, taking nearly one hundred years from the days when, under British colonial rule, the roots of apartheid were established.

Under Britain in 1900, fifty years before apartheid was formally institutionalized in South Africa, most of its features were already in place in the bustling gold-rush city of Johannesburg. By then Africans were prevented from walking on the pavements, had to carry 'pass' booklets to work in the city, could not use buses and trains designated for whites, were dreadfully exploited in the gold mines and had no political rights.

Today everyone says they were against apartheid. And doubtless many were. But some *did* things about it; others *didn't*.

The international anti-apartheid struggle was for most of its life engaged in a big, hard fight. Protests to stop whites-only Springbok rugby tours in the 1970s provoked fierce anger, especially in Britain, New Zealand and Australia. Yet, as Nelson Mandela confirmed to me after his release, the country's total sporting isolation was a key factor in making white South Africans realise they had to change.

Demands for trade and economic sanctions were also fiercely resisted, yet their partial implementation eventually helped propel the white business community in the late 1980s to demand radical change of the apartheid government from which they had so long and so profitably benefitted.

Hundreds of thousands of citizens across the world supported Mandela's fight for freedom. Courageous archbishops—such as

Britain's Trevor Huddleston, Ambrose Reeves and David Shepherd—led from both the pulpit and the street. Grannies boycotted South African oranges. Students forced Barclays Bank off their university campuses and then to withdraw from South Africa. Trade unionists worldwide gave solidarity. In the 1980s, the Black Caucus in the US Congress forced a change of policy under President Reagan and a decisive implementation of loan sanctions.

And in response, anti-apartheid activists were attacked. Inside the country, imprisonment, banning, torture and death were common. Leaders in exile were assassinated, as was Dulcie September in Paris and Ruth First in Maputo. (Ruth received a letter bomb of the kind sent to me in London in June 1972, which fortunately had a technical fault and did not explode.)

On every possible opportunity when he was free, Mandela thanked anti-apartheid campaigners across the world for freeing him and his people. Although his generosity to former opponents was legendary—old foes became new friends; former adversaries, admirers—he never forgot who was on his side and who wasn't.

Sadly, great causes, from slavery abolitionists to suffragettes and anti-apartheid campaigners, are invariably unpopular at the very time they most need support—only to be glorified, some even sanctified, once they have triumphed.

Although the majority in the British Parliament and the US Congress—and their governments of the day—opposed him and the ANC's freedom struggle for almost the entire period he was imprisoned, Mandela remained a democratic constitutionalist with an almost touching faith in parliamentary democracy. And that even though, by force of circumstance—the suppression of his African National Congress's nonviolent campaign for over sixty years—he had to become a freedom fighter, to lead an underground campaign of guerrilla activity similar to the French resistance against the Nazis.

His subsequent capacity for forgiveness is what made him the absolutely critical figure in the eventual liberation of his country, first during secret negotiations in the late 1980s from prison with his white oppressors in government, and then after his release.

On being elected president in 1994, he was acutely concerned at how close South Africa had come to civil war and subsequently insisted to his African National Congress at a private gathering of struggle veterans, '*You mustn't compromise your principles, but you mustn't humiliate the opposition. No one is more dangerous than one who is humiliated*'.

Some twenty years later, amid deep anger about the corruption and cronyism that flourished under Jacob Zuma's presidency, Mandela's message to his senior party activists in 1993 became poignantly pertinent to many South Africans and former anti-apartheid activists internationally: '*If the ANC does to you what the apartheid government did to you, then you must do to the ANC what you did to the apartheid government*'.

· 1 ·

Roots

*B*ut where did apartheid come from? How could a minority suppress the vast majority of South Africans simply because their skin color wasn't white? Mandela's people were and are the indigenous black people of the southern tip of Africa that came to be known as South Africa. It was their homeland. They farmed the countryside, they fished in the rivers and they moved their livestock over the mountains onto the plains and down through the valleys. The story of how that world was thrown upside down, how the people who used to be its masters became its slaves, goes back four centuries to when the first permanent white settlers from Europe, seeking a new life, landed at the Cape of Good Hope and found a land populated by Nelson Mandela's ancestors.

In 1652, the Dutch East India Company established the first settlement there, on the southwestern tip of Africa, to supply fresh food to the ships sailing to the Indies and back. Further bands of whites followed: Huguenot refugees from France in 1688 and later German immigrants. The Afrikaner people (who nearly three centuries later became the architects of apartheid) derived mainly from these three white ethnic groups.

In the Western Cape was the land of the indigenous nomadic herdsmen, the Khoikhoi (or Hottentots), which was progressively expropriated by the settlers. Eventually they, together with Malay

1

slaves from the Dutch East Indies and the offspring of mixed-race marriages, became the Cape Coloured people (or "Coloureds").

The other indigenous inhabitants, the San hunter-gatherers (Bushmen), were virtually eliminated by being hunted down and killed by whites. Additionally, from 1860 Indian indentured labor was imported by white entrepreneurs to work the sugarcane plantations in Natal, and they formed another significant racial group.

After Britain annexed the Cape in 1806, British settlement grew.

In 1820, some five thousand immigrants, including my mother's ancestors, were settled along the "white" side of the Fish River, about five hundred miles (800 km) east of the Cape, as a bulwark against the black chiefdoms (including Mandela's) that occupied most of the remaining area of the country.

By the 1830s, many Afrikaners (Boers) had become dissatisfied with British rule in the Cape. A major reason was the abolition of slavery, which for generations had provided the economic basis for Boer agriculture, together with the low compensation to slave owners paid by the British. So, in what became known as the "Great Trek", they moved north-eastward into black territory, using the advantage conferred by their guns and horses to subdue any black chiefdoms that resisted them, and eventually established their own independent Boer states. Ultimately, almost the whole of the land of what is now known as South Africa had been expropriated and was under white dominance.

The home of the Zulu people, Natal, on the east coast and north of the lands inhabited by Mandela's Xhosa-speaking people, came under British rule in 1845, and most Boers living there then moved north into two Boer states: the Orange Free State in the middle and Transvaal to the north. Later, however, when the British attempted to interfere with the running of the two states, the First Boer War broke out. Britain was defeated and made peace in 1881.

Meanwhile, in 1871, diamonds had been discovered in the Cape near the border with the Orange Free State, and they attracted a large influx of workers including blacks. This was followed in 1886 by the discovery of vast gold reserves in the Transvaal. Huge numbers of black workers from the many traditional African communities, as well as white immigrants from Europe, were drawn into these two Boer republics.

So, by the beginning of the Second Boer War, in 1899, South Africa consisted of two British colonies—the Cape and Natal—plus the independent Boer (Afrikaner) republics of the Orange Free State and the Transvaal. This Second Boer War resulted from Britain's wish to gain control of the northern gold mines (under the pretext of obtaining the vote for the foreigners who had flocked in to work them). It was a bloody conflict, finally ending with the defeat of the Boers in 1902; during it were established the first concentration camps. The British moved Boer families off the farms that provided bases for the marauding Boer guerrillas, crowding them into camps where sanitary conditions were primitive and disease was rife. Some twenty-six thousand Afrikaner women and children died, leaving an understandably deep scar on the Afrikaner psyche that still endures.

However, despite Britain's victory, Afrikaner nationalism would not be extinguished. The treaty that ended the war led to negotiations and the eventual granting of South Africa's independence in 1910. Under the Act of Union, political equality was given to all whites, but restrictions on the rights of blacks, Indians and Coloureds continued. So the conquest of the country ended with whites occupying 88 percent of the land they had chosen to farm and settle (and that just happened to contain all the country's known natural resources). The main black chiefdoms, such as Nelson Mandela's Thembu (part of the Xhosa-speaking people), were shouldered aside into scattered and poor pockets of land away from the "white" areas and called "native reserves".

The 1913 Natives Land Act, a cornerstone of South Africa's racist legislation, prevented blacks from acquiring land in "white" areas—all but 13 percent of the country. The act also enabled the eviction of "surplus natives" who had lived on "white" farms before their acquisition by the white owner. As a result, thousands of black families were driven off farms to wander homeless and starving. Blacks also lived in squalid townships called "locations" outside the urban areas. The main body of Indian people was in Natal, and most Coloureds were in the Western Cape; all of them lived in deprived conditions, albeit better than blacks.

—

Out of this history of gradual white domination of a traditional black African land developed apartheid with all its misery, oppression and injustice. Rejecting ancestral divisions and demanding equal rights and justice for all "Africans" (blacks, the indigenous people), Mandela's African National Congress was established in 1912. The first gathering opened with the hymn "Nkosi Sikelel' iAfrika" (God bless Africa), which became the ANC's national anthem; its flag, adopted in 1925, was black for the people, green for the land and gold for the resources.

Mandela's story is an extraordinary one and an inspiration for humanity: from barefoot herd boy to world leader, from freedom fighter to revered statesman and from prisoner to president.

· 2 ·

Grooming a Chief

$\mathscr{B}$orn Rolihlahla ("troublemaker") Mandela on July 18, 1918, Mandela was a Thembu, one of the groups of the Xhosa-speaking people in the Transkei Native Reserve, some five hundred miles (800 km) east of Cape Town and six hundred miles (965 km) south of Johannesburg.

It was a country of rolling hills, green grass, rondavels (round thatched huts) and herd boys driving cattle and sheep to graze. But by then it was overpopulated with eroded soil that could only sustain scattered groups of scrawny livestock and sporadic crops of maize, so most young men were obliged to leave and work in the white towns outside the reserves.

Gadla Henry Mphakanyiswa (Henry), his father, was a hereditary chief in the Madiba clan of the Thembu. Mandela's mother, Nosekeni Fanny, was the third of Henry's four wives in the ancestral kraal (group of huts), with its own fields, livestock and vegetables in the village of Mvezo. Each wife had her own kraal some distance from the others, and Henry would rotate his time between them.

In 1919, Mandela's father was removed from his chieftainship by a white magistrate for not showing sufficient respect, and the family moved away to the nearby village of Qunu. There the children's lives revolved around the three round huts of their mother's

5

kraal—one for sleeping, one for cooking and one for storing food. There were no beds or tables, only mats. Boys like Mandela spent the day herding cattle in the veld (fields); girls and mothers fetched water, tilled land and prepared food, with the main meal shared in the evening. Mandela thrived among the extended family of step-mothers, half-brothers and half-sisters.

The Transkei . . . is a beautiful country of rolling hills, fertile valleys and a thousand rivers and streams. . . . It was in the fields that I learned how to knock birds out of the sky with a slingshot, to gather wild honey and fruits and edible roots, to drink warm, sweet milk straight from the udder of a cow; to swim in the clear, cold streams and to catch fish.

. . . From these days I date my love of the veld, of open spaces, the simple beauties of nature, the clean line of the horizon.

His mother converted to Methodism, and, aged seven, he was sent to the local mission school, where his teacher gave him a new first name of Nelson. He became known simply as Nelson Mandela and, to his close friends, as Madiba (the name of his chiefdom). He was the only one in his family to go to school.

Tragedy struck when he was a child: his father died, having entrusted Mandela to the care of his cousin and friend Jongintaba, regent of the Thembu people. In 1927, Mandela was taken to live with the regent at the "Great Place" of Mqhekezweni. Also as the head of the Madiba clan, Jongintaba presided over the Thembus as acting king and paramount chief.

The Great Place was accessible only over a rough dirt road

and was a settlement of two plain houses facing a group of ronda-vels, with a garden between, a school building and some huts beyond. But people from all over Thembuland came miles on foot or horseback to consult the regent, who became Mandela's father figure. His son Justice, four years Mandela's elder, was to be the young Nelson's role model for the next decade.

He was brought up there within the African concept of human brotherhood, or *ubuntu*, which described a quality of mutual responsibility and compassion. Africans defined this as a contrast to the individualism and restlessness of the whites. One of the old chiefs whom Mandela visited said that the unity and peace of the Xhosa people had been broken by the coming of the white man, who had divided them, dispossessed them and undermined their ubuntu, which Mandela regarded as part of the general philosophy of serving one's fellow men and women.

The history of his people was very much alive when Mandela was a child, and old men could remember the time when the Xhosa-speaking groups were still undefeated and they retained their distinctive culture and language. But over the course of a hundred years in the eighteenth and nineteenth centuries and nine Xhosa wars, the British had gradually deprived the Xhosas of their independence and lands. Successive leaders were banished to Robben Island, and after the Union of South Africa came into being in 1910, all the Xhosas, and other groups, faced increasing control by white magistrates.

When Mandela was sixteen, in 1934, the regent decided it was time for him "to become a man," only achieved in the Xhosa tradition by circumcision. Males not circumcised could not inherit their father's wealth, marry or officiate at chiefdom rituals. He went with twenty-five other Thembu boys, led by his friend Justice, to the traditional place for circumcision of future Thembu kings, which was two grass huts in a remote valley near the Mbashe River.

At dawn they were escorted to the river to bathe, Mandela painfully remembering the whole episode: '*Circumcision is a trial of bravery and stoicism; a man must suffer in silence. I felt as if fire was shoot-ing through my veins; the pain was so intense that I buried my chin in my chest'*. The recently circumcised boys lived in the two huts as their wounds healed, and women were prevented from seeing them.

At a ceremony afterward, Mandela heard the main speaker, Chief Meligqili, denounce their predicament as a people:

> We Xhosas, and all Black South Africans, are a conquered people. We are slaves in our own country. We are tenants on our own soil. We have no strength, no power, no control over our own destiny in the land of our birth. . . . The abilities, the promise of these young men will be squandered in their attempt to eke out a living doing the simplest, most mindless chores for the White man.

It was a sacred time; I felt happy and fulfilled taking part in my people's customs and ready to make the transition from boyhood to manhood. It was a period of quietude, a kind of spiritual preparation for the trials of manhood that lay ahead.

This powerful call for freedom and independence made an impact on the teenager: '*Without exactly understanding why, the chief's words began to work on me. He had sown a seed, and though I let that seed lie dormant for a long season, it eventually began to grow'*.

Mandela was still very much rooted in his Thembu group, proud that he was different to non-Thembu classmates he encoun-tered when he was then sent to the remote rural Methodist board-ing school of Clarkebury, where the regent and Justice had been educated. By then it was the biggest educational centre in Them-buland, a coeducational boarding school with sports fields and ten-nis courts, and he was introduced to a whole new world.

But he was surprised not to be treated with the deference to which he had been accustomed in his home villages: '*I quickly realized that I had to make my way on the basis of my ability, not my heritage*'. When Mandela shook the principal's hand, it was the first white one he'd ever shaken. He passed his junior certificate in two years and then, aged nineteen, was sent in 1937 to Healdtown, a bigger Methodist institution, which was almost as remote to reach as Clarkebury and was also coeducational.

Mandela was therefore inducted into Christianity and was influenced by the school's strict discipline, mental training and avoidance of thrills and distractions. The white teachers kept aloof from the black teachers and ate separately, and boys and girls were widely separated outside classrooms but attended mixed dinners every Sunday, wearing their best clothes. Attending a boarding school also introduced Mandela to pajamas, flush toilets and showers.

But although his awareness of the harsh predicament of his Xhosa people had been roused by the speeches of Thembu chiefs at community gatherings, he first heard of the ANC at Healdtown and was not interested in politics. His main interest outside his studies was sport: he took up boxing and football and especially enjoyed the discipline and solitude of long-distance running—which would stand him in good stead decades later.

Mandela graduated from Healdtown in 1938 and a year later, prompted by his regent, went to the South African Native College of Fort Hare, a few miles away, which was the only black university in South Africa. With just 150 students, it had been set up in 1916 by Scottish missionaries, and it attracted students from all over Africa. He found a few Indians and Coloureds but mainly the intellectual elite of black South Africans and only a handful of women students, often cleverer than the men—something that surprised Mandela whose traditional upbringing had been about the alleged superiority of men.

Mandela, however, was never at the heart of the Fort Hare intellectuals, who included many of his friends and relations. The student body brought together both royal and mission families, and when he arrived as a fresher of twenty-one he was daunted by the sophistication and confidence of his seniors. The regent had bought him his first suit: '*Double breasted and gray, the suit made me feel grown up and sophisticated*', he remembered. However, the regent gave him no pocket money, and he had something to spend only because a relative shared a parental allowance.

Although never arrogant, Mandela was treated as a young prince, with a special status even in Fort Hare's intellectual atmosphere, which inspired both respect and resentment. Some of his friends were already active in politics, and he met Oliver Tambo (much later to be a fellow ANC leader) there. He saw Tambo and others as more able, and his immediate ambition was to be a court interpreter, with a degree and a position in the community that would enable him to support his family. There was no inkling here of the dominant political leader Mandela would later become.

But he had a rebellious streak: in his second year, he was elected to lead student protests against the Spartan and terrible meals they were served. Here there were signs of the stubbornness, uncompromising strength of principle and resilience he would later display. When five of the students elected with him to lead the protests backed down, Mandela alone held out, feeling that was his moral duty as an elected representative; he was also upset about what he saw as divide-and-rule "trickery" by the university principal. The principal tried to dissuade him, stating that otherwise he would be expelled and urging him to sleep on it.

Mandela spent a restless night:

Was I sabotaging my academic career over an abstract moral principle that mattered very little? . . . . I had taken a stand, and I did not want to appear a fraud in the eyes of my fellow students. At the same time, I did not want to throw away my career at Fort Hare . . . . I knew it was foolhardy for me to leave Fort

*Hare, but when I needed to compromise, some-
thing inside would not let me.*

He refused to back down and was expelled, returning to the Great
Place, where he was met by a furious regent and instructed to apologize and go back to Fort Hare, which he refused to do, instead
resuming his old life at home. But a few weeks later came another
shock turn in his life. He and Justice were summoned to see the
regent, who informed them gravely '*I fear that I am not much longer
for this world, and before I journey to the land of my ancestors, it is my duty
to see my two sons properly married. I have accordingly arranged unions for
both of you*'.

Despite being aware that the regent was acting in strict accor-
dance with Thembu law and custom, they both felt helpless at this
devastating news, hardly reassured by hearing that the girls were
from "good families." Mandela's bride-to-be was the daughter of a
Thembu priest.

The marriages were to take place right away. It was 1941 and
a decisive moment. He and Justice resolved that their only alternative was to flee to distant Johannesburg. With no money, they sold
two of the regent's prized oxen to a local trader and caught a train.
Through various trials and tribulations—not least ingeniously overcoming tight restrictions on travel by Africans—they eventually
approached the big city, late in the evening, dazzled by the glinting
lights.

Mandela was twenty-three, still unpolitical and relatively
unsophisticated. He remembered:

*I was terribly excited to see the city I had heard
about since I was a child, . . . a city of dreams,
. . . a city of danger and of opportunity. . . .*

*I had reached the end of what seemed like
a long journey, but it was actually the very*

beginning of a much longer and more trying journey that would test me in ways that I could not then have imagined.

He had been groomed—but not to become the sort of chief he had ever envisaged.

· 3 ·

Second Class

*W*hen he arrived in Johannesburg, Mandela—as he later self-deprecatingly called himself—was a "country boy," albeit educated way beyond almost all of his peers still herding livestock back at home. He found a bustling city, surrounded by gold mines. In this commercial hub of the country, blacks were its engine but without rights and so badly exploited. Segregation was strict—whites supervising black miners toiling for poverty wages deep in the bowels of the earth. Hostels for the black workers consisted of concrete bunks without mattresses, and just inches apart, stretching along bleak, single-sex barracks. Women and children were hundreds of miles away at home, to be visited once or twice yearly on pilgrimages to their home areas.

Mandela's temporary stay with a cousin was to prove significant because it led to him being introduced to Walter Sisulu, a young businessman and influential local leader of the ANC, which he had joined in 1940. Sisulu, later to be ANC deputy president and a fellow prisoner on Robben Island, also came from the Transkei. He lacked Mandela's group status but had tremendous inner confidence and was to become the most important political influence in Mandela's life and a lifelong friend. Six years older than Mandela, Sisulu was part of a small black estate agency in the city and was able to give Mandela a job, provide financial help to enable him to finish his BA degree by correspondence at Fort Hare, and then introduce him to a white legal firm to which he was articled.

Mandela found a room in Alexandra, a slum township northeast of Johannesburg. Known as the "Dark City" because it had no electricity, Alexandra was a lawless place, yet it had a strong sense of community. Mandela boarded in a small house with six children crowded in, but he was relatively comfortable given the appalling conditions in the township. Although he was allocated a tin-roofed shack added at the back of the house, with a dirt floor and no running water or heat, he said it occupied '*a treasured place in my heart. It was the first place I had ever lived away from home*'.

Life was cheap; the gun and the knife ruled at night. . . . Police raids were a regular feature. The police routinely arrested masses of people for pass violations, possession of liquor and failure to pay the poll tax. On almost every corner there were shebeens, illegal saloons where home-brewed beer was served. In that first year, I learnt more about poverty than I did in all my childhood days.

Dirt tracks passed for roads, with smelly pools of filthy water everywhere, a squall of polluted air from coal braziers hung over the place and dirty, hungry children roaming around.

Mandela normally walked six miles (9.5 km) to and then from work to save the bus fare and often went for days with hardly any food and without changing his clothes. A suit given to him by his white boss at the law firm lasted five years and was worn daily.

'*In the end, there were more patches than suit*'. Yet in that poverty-stricken life he made real friends, was given his only hot meal of the week on Sundays by his landlord, and started growing

in confidence as he found he no longer needed the royal connec-
tions that had sustained him before. He also mixed daily with other
groups in the hustle and bustle of Alexandra.

His whole worldview had changed radically, something he
realised on returning home for the funeral of the regent in mid-
1942. When Justice stayed behind to succeed as regent, Mandela
felt guilty at abandoning his roots and family in Thembuland, but
he felt his destiny lay in his new life, completing his studies.
Proudly, he graduated at Fort Hare at the end of 1942.

Gaur Radebe, an influential black clerk in his law firm, had
taken Mandela under his wing, over time persuading him during
their regular conversations that education was essential but insufficient as an engine for change. The only way forward for the
oppressed black majority, hemmed in everywhere by the system of
racial division and discrimination that had been developing
remorselessly for generations, was the African National Congress
and the Communist Party, argued Radebe, who took Mandela
along to ANC meetings.

August 1943 proved another turning point for Mandela, then
aged twenty-five. Ten thousand people marched in support of a
bus boycott in Alexandra, demanding a halt to a steep rise in fares:
'*This campaign had a great effect on me. In a small way, I had departed
from my role as an observer and become a participant. I found that to march
with one's people was exhilarating and inspiring. But I was also impressed
by the boycott's effectiveness: after nine days, during which the buses ran
empty, the company reinstated the fare to four pence*'.

Walter Sisulu lent Mandela money to buy a new suit for his
graduation ceremony when he returned to Fort Hare early in 1943.
There, colleagues and relatives from his youth tried to draw him
back to the Transkei, but he resisted and continued his work in
Johannesburg and in politics. Again with Sisulu's help, Mandela
enrolled to study for a law degree part time at the University of the
Witwatersrand. Known as "Wits", it was a white university that
admitted some nonwhite students. There Mandela met whites

("Europeans") in a completely different relationship from the customary white/black, master/servant role that was then the norm in South Africa. It was as novel an encounter for them as it was for him, the only black student in the law faculty.

He mixed with young white and Indian student political activists of his own age who drew him further into a ferment of political discussion, their circle widening outside the university. Many of them were later to form the vanguard of the future resistance. Mandela was struck forcefully that whites enjoying a privileged life were willing to align themselves with the oppressed majority and make sacrifices they did not need to.

He did not perform well academically, perhaps because politics had started to dominate his life: '*I cannot pinpoint a moment when I became politicized, when I knew that I would spend my life in the liberation struggle. . . . I had no epiphany, no single revelation, no moment of truth, but a steady accumulation of a thousand sights, and a thousand indignities, produced in me a rebelliousness, an anger, a desire to fight the system that imprisoned my people*'.

A more militant spirit of African nationalism and black empowerment, rather than reliance on British colonial paternalism, was stirring among younger ANC members. With Sisulu, Mandela became part of a small group who wanted to form an ANC Youth League, pressing for mass actions. They felt the old tactics were not effective, the system was getting worse almost daily, and the ANC needed to be transformed into a mass movement for change.

Mandela joined the ANC in 1944, and that April the ANC Youth League was formally launched with Mandela, Sisulu and Oliver Tambo on the executive committee. But Mandela still felt '*a certain insecurity, feeling politically backward*' compared with Sisulu and the others. He was also working full time and studying part time, so had little free time.

Domestically, his life was changing too and becoming more demanding. He left Alexandra and moved close to Sisulu in Orlando township. In 1944, he met and married Sisulu's cousin Evelyn Mase, recently arrived from the Transkei to become a nurse. Evelyn (unlike the agnostically inclined Mandela) was from a devout mission background and not interested in politics.

A year later, in 1945, their son Thembi was born. Mandela was pleased to have fulfilled what he described as '*one of the basic responsibilities of a Xhosa male*'—to perpetuate the Mandela name and his Madiba clan. Earlier, they had moved to their own house in Orlando West, another proud moment: '*A man is not a man until he has a house of his own*', he believed. It was a standard township house built by the municipality for African workers in the city; it was tiny with a tin roof, concrete floor filled almost entirely by the bed, a bucket toilet outside and paraffin lamps. The family had to wash from a tap in the yard. The following year, a daughter was born who sadly died after nine months. Unusually for a male of that era, Mandela helped with the shopping and bathing the babies, and sometimes cooked. He was highly organized—rose very early, jogged for a few miles and then left for the day at work.

This was a time of big social and political change, with a growing global dimension to the ANC's perspective. The Second World War had divided South Africa's white population, its Parliament voting only narrowly by just thirteen votes to support the Allies, with Afrikaners siding heavily with the Nazis. Some of the Afrikaans leaders, including a later prime minister, John Vorster, were interned for pro-Nazi activity including sabotage. However, Africans and Coloureds joined South African regiments and took part in the Allied world effort.

In 1946, two events jolted Mandela into increased politicization.

First, dreadfully exploited black miners followed their African Mineworkers Union into a strike. More than seventy thousand downed tools for more pay and better food and conditions. With government support, the mining companies forced the workers back down the mines with bayonets, killing nine and wounding hundreds, shocking Mandela. More than fifty men were arrested for incitement and then prosecuted for sedition. ANC elders blamed the communists for provoking a premature test of strength.

But the ANC Youth Leaguers criticized the elders for not calling a general strike in sympathy. The crushing of the strike made fools of the ANC "Old Guard", who had put their faith in the government of Jan Smuts, an allegedly patrician white prime minister, close to the British and highly regarded internationally.

The second event was when the Smuts government failed another test. In 1946, it introduced the Asiatic Land Tenure Act, the "Indian Ghetto Act," which banned the sale of any more land to Indian South Africans. Two thousand protesters went to jail, including their leaders. Mandela was impressed by the mass action of the Indians, in contrast to what he saw as the inertia of the ANC and of his fellow Africans. He was now meeting many Indians and white communists, including Ahmed Kathrada (the latter to be a key confidant of Mandela's) and Ruth First, a notable activist.

Mandela, nevertheless, remained opposed to closer political cooperation with the Indians as he was convinced that only separate African and Indian "congresses" could be effective in mobilizing their masses, and he worried that the Indians might control the ANC for their own purposes. However, the independence of India in 1947 was a powerful encouragement for the struggle in South Africa, because it showed that an established ruling power could be defeated by unified organized mass movement, and one using Gandhi's tactics of nonviolent direct action.

He also distrusted the Communist Party, which had been formed in 1920 as a white party but by the 1930s was recruiting more nonwhite members and by now was the only nonracial party in South Africa. The ANC already included many communist members, and while Mandela got on with them individually, he remained suspicious that their party with its tight discipline and ties to Moscow could manipulate the ANC.

Although Mandela moved up a notch to join the executive of the Transvaal ANC in 1947, he was still not a leading player in practice or in spirit. In April that year, the British royal family arrived and spent thirty-five days touring South Africa. The celebrations were boycotted by the ANC and the Youth League, but

Mandela, with his royal background, did not join the boycott out of respect for the British monarchy as a long-lasting institution.

—

Then came a cathartic and ominous shift in South Africa's trajectory. In May 1948, Jan Smuts's largely English United Party lost the whites-only general election. Especially because Smuts (like Churchill in Britain, who also lost its general election) was a popular war leader, it was a shock to many, including Mandela who was *'stunned and dismayed'*. The victor was Dr. Daniel Malan's largely Afrikaner National Party, which had a much more fundamentalist ideological commitment to rigid separation of the races—called apartheid. The Nationalists' pro-Nazi and anti-Jewish attitudes were played down, and they believed themselves to be *'chosen by God to rule'*. The ANC saw the election as a choice between two evils, and educated Africans in Orlando despised the Afrikaners whom they knew only as train drivers, ticket collectors and policemen. The Afrikaners had an independent culture with a powerful nationalism, its own Calvinist religion, and continued grievances against the English.

Malan's Nationalist government soon began reformulating the country's traditional racial divisions along rigid apartheid lines. Its legislative cornerstone, the Population Registration Act, provided an absurdly circuitous definition of "whiteness", Orwellian in character.

Under this act, all South Africans were processed by Race Classification Boards into their racial groups. If they were judged white or Coloured (Indians and Chinese were included with Coloureds), their obligatory identity card would contain a photograph, a signature, an identity number and a racial group. If judged to be black ("Bantu" in the new official jargon) and over the age of sixteen, the identify document—officially called the Reference Book—would specify in which particular urban area he or she had permission to be, whether permission had been granted to work there and for whom. The book would have to be signed by the employer every month and had to include tax receipts. Commonly known as a "pass", it had to be kept on the bearer's person twenty-four hours a day, and failure to produce it on demand by the police rendered blacks liable to arrest under the Pass Laws. It was a draconian mechanism to control every daily movement of Africans.

Residential segregation was deepened and enforced through a new Group Areas Act, which, on the basis of race, set out where individuals could live and with whom. If the person was judged white, this would not be of undue concern, since white areas comprised 88 percent of the country and included all the industrial and business areas, all the urban areas with their garden suburbs and swimming pools, and all the popular beauty spots and holiday resorts. If, however, the person was judged Coloured, living would be restricted to designated residential areas outside the towns, and commercial activities would be confined to these areas, although employment could be sought in the towns. Coloureds could also find—as Indian shopkeepers in the Transvaal did—that they were uprooted from premises that they and their families had occupied for half a century and then banished miles away to the bare veld, to make way for whites.

A White person means a person who:
a) in appearance is obviously a White person and who is not generally accepted as a Coloured person; or
b) is generally accepted as a White person and is not in appearance obviously not a White person.
from the Population Registration Act, 1950

People who were judged black would find themselves further classified into a particular chiefdom group, determining—subject to the permission of the local chief—in which chiefdom reserve they would have residential rights. To live outside this reserve (which they might never have seen or have any knowledge of, and which could be as much as 1,000 miles/1,600 kilometers away) required the permission of a white official, entered in the pass. This permission, which was not automatically granted and could be withdrawn at any time, would be for a specified area only, usually a town. Furthermore, blacks could not remain for more than seventy-two hours in any area other than that for which they had specific permission, without another permit.

With the exception of domestic servants who were allowed to "live in" with white families (albeit in separate accommodation often attached to a garage), all blacks residing in an urban area were obliged to live in segregated municipal townships, usually separated from the town proper by a buffer strip of open country. Children over the age of eighteen could not live with their parents in these townships without a permit, and in the larger townships, which were segregated on group lines, a wife of a different group was required to have a permit to live with her husband. Every urban area had a curfew—from 11:00 p.m. in the larger towns and 9:30 p.m. in the smaller ones—after which no black could be on the streets without a special pass signed by a white.

Whereas previously under largely English white rule South Africa's society had been riddled with racism, now its whole structure—from the very bottom to the very top—was institutionally organized according to the evil doctrine of apartheid. Mandela and his colleagues in the ANC were now experiencing an altogether different level of threat as they tried to represent their long-suffering people. If the conditions in which they lived had been bad, they were about to get terrible.

—

In 1948, Mandela visited Cape Town for the first time, staying for three months, where he met leading members of the Trotskyite "Unity Movement", including Africans and Coloureds. He was surprised that they seemed more hostile to the ANC than to the government and thought that their doctrinaire insistence on non-collaboration with any other organization including the ANC was only an excuse for '*doing nothing*'.

Mandela and the ANC Youth League had prepared a plan of action aimed at organizing mass protest and passive resistance against the government, like Gandhi's in India, and in November 1949 they went to see the then ANC president Alfred Xuma privately at his home. They argued that the ANC was too docile and now had no alternative but to adopt the Youth League's plan of mass action including strikes, boycotts, stay-at-homes, civil disobedience and noncooperation. Militant but nonviolent direct action was the only way of combating the relentless and ruthless march of apartheid.

They also warned Xuma that, if he did not support them, they would vote against his presidency at the annual ANC conference in December. He showed them the door.

> *I was never an outstanding boxer. . . . I had neither enough power to compensate for my lack of speed nor enough speed to make up for my lack of power. I did not enjoy the violence of boxing so much as the science of it. . . . My main interest was in training; I found the rigorous exercise to be an excellent outlet for tension and stress. . . . It was a way of losing myself in something that was not the struggle. After an evening's work-out I would wake up ready to take up the fight again.*

But at the conference the Youth League had the majority support, Xuma was ousted, their plan was enthusiastically adopted and

Sisulu was appointed as full-time paid secretary. Mandela, Tambo and other Youth Leaguers joined the national executive, and in 1950 Mandela was elected as president of the Youth League.

Although politics was now his main preoccupation, by this time Mandela was beginning to earn money as a practicing lawyer, was a township big shot, owned a car, ate in the few downtown restaurants that admitted Africans, took great trouble with his clothes and had the confidence of a man about town, with great presence and charm. But he remained an aristocrat rather than a commoner, and one who did not approve of hard liquor. He was six foot two inches (1.88 meters), physically imposing and a keen heavyweight boxer, training on weekdays at a local gym in Orlando.

Also in 1950, the government made the Communist Party illegal with its Suppression of Communism Act, which marked the beginning of the end of the rule of law. However, "statutory communism" was defined much more widely than simply being in the party. Essentially, you were a "communist" if a government minister decreed you to be; no reason need be given, and there was no charge, trial or right of appeal. The penalties included being "banned" from membership of organizations.

A banning order, among other things, confined banned people to a specified area and prohibited them from entering educational premises and courts of law. The ban, as our family was also to discover, prohibited banned persons from communicating with one another, or being publicly quoted. They were prohibited from attending gatherings of more than one other person and were required to report to the police once a week. A more extreme form of banning was "house arrest" under which they became nonpersons.

Although the act badly disrupted the growing resistance, it also brought many communists much closer to the ANC's young activists like Mandela and moved them both towards joint action, Oliver Tambo's words proving prophetic: '*Today it is the Communist Party. Tomorrow our trade unions and the ANC*'.

In line with the ANC's new policy of mass action, a one-day stoppage of work on May Day 1950 was organized, proving a great success, with more than half the workforce staying at home. However, ferocious police attacks and shootings caused riots, resulting in eighteen Africans being killed and more than thirty injured. For Mandela that day was an eye opener: both the ruthlessness of the police and the grassroots backing given to the strike. He and Sisulu were also impressed at the hard work of one young Indian especially, Ahmed Kathrada, who became a firm friend. So apartheid laws intended to separate people were instead driving them together.

Mandela was becoming increasingly prominent as he continued to change, thinking more seriously about political theory and reading voraciously, including Marxist books. He now accepted that the ANC needed allies and that Indians and communists were the only ones available, as Africans moved into a new era of resistance.

Yet the brilliant British journalist (and years later Mandela's close friend and authorized biographer) Anthony Sampson recalled his perception at the time: '*I would love to recollect that I recognized Mandela from the start as a true leader of his people, destined to change the course of history. But in truth at that time I sadly underestimated him: he seemed to me too flashy and vain, with his immaculate suits and his wide smile*'. However valid or not this assessment was then, it later proved to be fundamentally wrong.

· 4 ·

Freedom Fighter

$\mathscr{B}$y the early 1950s Johannesburg's townships were the magnets for black South Africans flooding in from rural areas and their introduction to a newfound westernized world. Politicians and intellectuals lived side by side with factory workers, teachers and gangsters. The townships, which included Orlando, were of uniform matchbox houses and were later all included in the area called Soweto (an acronym for South Western Townships).

Having blacks in its increasingly vicelike grip, the government next targeted the Coloured population. A new law took Coloured voters off the common voters roll they had enjoyed with whites for more than a century, reducing their rights as they were forced to elect separate representatives. Outraged, Coloureds protested in a big demonstration in Cape Town in March 1951, following this a few weeks later with a strike that closed shops and kept children away from school.

Mandela and his close comrades were impressed by this new militancy, with Coloureds now following Indians and Africans into activism. Walter Sisulu immediately saw the opportunity for greater coordination between the groups, and he suggested the potential for a national civil disobedience campaign. Although Mandela supported this, and despite slowly coming to embrace communist activists, he remained suspicious of Indian influence, arguing that many rank-and-file Africans felt Indian shopkeepers and businesses exploited black workers. The ANC should go it alone, he insisted. But Sisulu strongly disagreed, and Mandela's position was defeated at an ANC executive.

He and his close leadership colleagues were, however, already moving onto a new phase of the struggle. In December 1951, when the ANC held its annual conference, Sisulu produced a "Defiance Campaign" report, which was enthusiastically accepted. In January 1952, Mandela helped draft a letter to Prime Minister Daniel Malan demanding the repeal of the "six unjust laws" that imposed Pass Laws and institutionalized apartheid. If he refused, they would embark on their Defiance Campaign. Malan's response was dismissive: the laws were '*not oppressive and degrading, but protective*', and he made clear that the state would crush any defiance.

Mandela, who retained an old-fashioned sense of courtesy in the way he behaved towards others, regarded Malan's very curtness as a "declaration of war". He became volunteer in chief for the Defiance Campaign and was the main speaker at a rally in Durban attended by around ten thousand people. He roused the expectant crowd by saying the campaign would make history as the first real example of mass resistance to growing oppression. Significantly— and in a departure from his previous stance—he urged unity between Africans, Coloureds and Indians, saying it was now happening on the ground.

On the ANC freedom day, June 26, in Boksburg, he went with Sisulu to observe fifty-two volunteers led by the Indian activist Nana Sita being arrested and jailed after walking into an African township without the necessary permits required for entry. That night the ANC held a meeting in Johannesburg, and volunteers walked out into the street after the 11:00 p.m. curfew for blacks and were arrested. Mandela had his first taste of detention when, as an observer, he was also arrested and spent two nights in jail, squashed in with fellow protesters.

This set the pattern for the 1952 Defiance Campaign. More than eight thousand people in the next five months went to jail for one to three weeks for marching into townships, entering whites-only railway entrances or carriages or being out after curfew, always peacefully.

But this very success proved toxic for the government, which was worried about the obvious unity in action between Africans, Indians and Coloureds. It provided an excuse for the imposition of even fiercer laws and more drastic penalties against intentional lawbreaking, punishable by up to three years in jail and flogging. Furthermore, on July 30, 1952, with the campaign at its height, there were nationwide raids on ANC offices, and Mandela was arrested under the Suppression of Communism Act, as were nineteen other campaign leaders. All went on trial in September and were sentenced to nine months' imprisonment with hard labor, albeit suspended for two years as the judge noted their peaceful intent.

In October, Mandela was overwhelmingly elected president of the Transvaal ANC, signifying his rising importance. But in December, with fifty-one other ANC leaders, he was banned for six months from attending any meeting or talking to more than one person at a time or for leaving Johannesburg without permission, which meant that his position as president had become illegal.

Although the Defiance Campaign had begun to peter out by the end of the year, it had given blacks a new confidence in their own strength, with the ANC's membership jumping from twenty thousand to one hundred thousand. Mandela also considered that the campaign had led to the formation of the nonracial Liberal Party in 1953 and to the Congress of Democrats (the latter essentially an organization of white ex-Communist Party members), both of which broadened the struggle into new layers of white society.

The campaign had also completely changed the character of the ANC; the more timid leaders were ousted, and a Zulu chief, Albert Luthuli, was elected president in December 1952, with Mandela elevated as his deputy. Mandela, however, was unable to participate because of his banning order, which also prevented him from attending his son's birthday party.

Nevertheless, he was exhilarated. The campaign, he felt, had been a huge success. The ANC had attracted mass support, with its activists hardened through encounters with the police, courts and prisons. '*The stigma usually associated with imprisonment had been removed*', he wrote. '*This was a significant achievement, for fear of imprisonment is a tremendous hindrance to a liberation struggle. From the Defiance Campaign onward, going to prison became a badge of honor for Africans*'.

The British high commissioner in South Africa and the Churchill government, both of which were still shaped by reactionary colonialist attitudes, were typically dismissive of the ANC. However, the Canadian high commissioner was more perceptive, reporting in February 1953, '*The ANC is a great deal more than a political party. Representing the great majority of articulate Africans in the Union, it is almost the parliament of a nation*'.

> *I nevertheless felt a great sense of accomplishment and satisfaction. . . . The campaign freed me from any lingering sense of doubt or inferiority I might still have felt; it liberated me from the feeling of being overwhelmed by the power and seeming invincibility of the White man and his institutions. . . . I had come of age as a freedom fighter.*

—

Now in his mid-thirties, Mandela at that time appeared to have a settled home life in Orlando, with his wife Evelyn running their matchbox house with dedication. But it was much less stable than those of his friends and mentors Walter Sisulu or Oliver Tambo.

Evelyn disapproved of his deepening political activity, and he realised that her religion (she had become a dedicated Jehovah's Witness) would not support his political career. Strains set into their marriage and, as later in his life, Mandela's public success belied private sorrow and disappointment, despite his immense love of family, people and friendship.

In August 1952, after he became a qualified attorney, he and Oliver Tambo established "Mandela and Tambo"—the first African law firm in the country. It shared a building with the ANC head-quarters. The two had a lot in common. Tambo was also from the rural Transkei, had a polygamous father, and had been expelled from Fort Hare. But otherwise he was Mandela's opposite: not gregarious and outward going, but quiet, academic and religious. Mandela respected Tambo's maturity and always listened to his advice, especially as his career at this time was contradictory—being both practicing lawyer and revolutionary politician.

Mandela spent much of his time in court, arguing in flamboyant style and then writing political speeches until late at night; Tambo stayed in the office doing much of the paperwork and in court behaved unobtrusively, relying on his knowledge of the law. The firm became the official attorneys to the ANC, and these attorneys were much in demand by black clients, including rural ones, who were always falling foul of the apartheid laws and were keen to be represented by a fellow African. To reach their desks in the morning they had to run the gauntlet of patient queues of people.

Mandela recalled why so many needed so much help at the time:

It was a crime to walk through a Whites-only door, a crime to ride a Whites-only bus, a crime to walk on a Whites-only beach, a crime to be on the streets after 11 pm, a crime not to have

*a pass book and a crime to have the wrong sig-
nature in that book, a crime to be unemployed
and a crime to be employed in the wrong place,
a crime to live in certain places and a crime to
have no place to live.*

It was in short a crime to be born with black skin, indeed to be an African.

When Mandela's six-month ban from attending meetings or leaving Johannesburg expired in June 1953, he drove to a small country town in the Orange Free State to represent a client, once again enjoying the wide open space of his rural youth. Despite his increasingly sophisticated and cosmopolitan lifestyle, smart suited and with his own American car, the trip reminded him he was '*still a country boy at heart*'.

However, he had hardly stepped into the local courthouse when waiting police officers served him with a fresh banning order, requiring him to resign from all organizations including the ANC for two years, and again restricting him to Johannesburg. He was forced to return there immediately, recognizing that, aged thirty-five, this was another turning point in his gradual emergence as a freedom fighter in the struggle, which had taken over his life. He would now have to become a clandestine operator, his work for the ANC circumventing the legal straitjacket imposed upon him, though the terms of his ban still enabled him to speak at public rallies in local areas like Soweto as long as they were not ANC events.

He was one of about a hundred ANC and trade union leaders, including the ANC president Albert Luthuli, to be banned, and the more Mandela thought about his predicament, the more he realised it was also a turning point for the liberation struggle as a whole.

Understanding that such bans would soon cripple the ANC

by restricting its leaders, contacts and activities, and expecting that the ANC would eventually itself be banned, Mandela worked out a plan—called the "M-Plan"—for the leaders to communicate quickly and secretly with each other by an underground network of cells.

In a presidential address delivered in his enforced absence as a banned person, he told attendees at the ANC's Transvaal conference in September 1953 that if they were unable to hold public meetings, they must hold them at work, in their factories, on trams and buses on the way home or in their villages and shanty towns. In Churchillian terms he insisted, '*Never surrender*'. He linked the South African struggle to others in Africa, citing revolutionary eruptions in Tunisia, Kenya and Rhodesia, and ended with a quotation from Jawaharlal Nehru, prime minister of recently independent India: '*There is no easy walk to freedom*', the title of Mandela's speech.

During this time a new confrontation came to a head. In line with apartheid's dictum that racial groups had to live separately—also a necessary mechanism for making the Pass Law controls work—the authorities had decided that the unique nonracial township of Sophiatown, four miles (6.5 km) from Johannesburg's white heartland, had to go. Originally intended as a white development, its location next to a rubbish dump put off many whites and the developer was forced to sell to anybody of any race who could be found.

Sophiatown was an overcrowded slum, one of South Africa's most cosmopolitan areas, and was the only part of the city where blacks could own freehold property. Black residents were to be forced to leave their homes for Soweto, many miles away, and given puny compensation. There was uproar locally, and for the ANC, this was a serious trial of strength. A major campaign against the removal was organized, supported by Father Trevor Huddleston, an English priest who later wrote *Naught for Your Comfort* (1956), an important book that stirred international concern.

On Sundays, the ANC organized rallies to mobilize resistance and Mandela was a speaker. His speeches were becoming more warlike, sounding more like a revolutionary than a lawyer, notably on December 13, 1953, at a big meeting in Soweto, where he roused the crowd with his force and passion. Indignant at the banning or arrest of local leaders and the growing repression by the police state, he '*overstepped the line*' as he later recalled. Nonviolent resistance was becoming "*useless*"; violence would be necessary to secure change.

Mandela may, as he reflected, have '*got carried away*', but the security officers listening duly noted what he said. And this significant new escalation in the struggle (cheered wildly by the crowd) was the fruit of both his frustration and his sober analysis of the difficulties of confronting such a seemingly ubiquitous state apparatus. The ANC's slogan for Sophiatown—"Over Our Dead Bodies"—reflected this and was boisterously chanted by platform speakers and people at the rallies over the following weeks. However, when it came to the crunch, the ANC pulled back. Disappointing younger activists, who were prepared to build barricades and use whatever weapons they could find—literally to resist "Over Our Dead Bodies"—ANC leaders urged restraint.

Early on the morning of February 9, 1954, thousands of police officers and soldiers cordoned off the township and ordered the dismantling of houses, and heavy trucks arrived to forcefully move out the tenants and their furniture. Mandela reflected ruefully, '*In the end Sophiatown died not to the sound of gunfire but to the sound of rumbling trucks and sledgehammers*'.

It was a bitter defeat with a huge impact upon the ANC. Mandela was self-critical about the mistakes they had made, acknowledging that rousing crowds and exciting young militants with talk of violent resistance was wrong when the ANC was not actually willing (or for that matter able) to carry it out. Nevertheless, it reinforced in him his conviction that armed and violent resistance was now their only option. '*Over and over again, we had used all the non-violent weapons in our arsenal—speeches, deputations, threats, marches, strikes, stay-aways, voluntary imprisonment—all to no avail, for whatever we did was met by an iron hand'*. Reflecting this, when Sisulu was invited to a communist youth festival in Romania, Mandela persuaded him also to visit China, which was an inspiration to liberation struggles worldwide. But Chinese communist leaders surprised them by warning against an armed struggle, arguing this should not be attempted until they were ready for it. Although Mandela accepted this, he remained convinced that such a struggle would indeed eventually become necessary.

Meanwhile, apartheid was marching on, step by step intruding into every facet of life, with the government determined to enforce racial segregation in all schools. The minister for education and apartheid fundamentalist, Hendrik Verwoerd, complained that the pre-apartheid system of schooling had misled blacks by showing them *'the green pastures of White society in which they are not allowed to graze'*. The 1953 Bantu Education Act, Verwoerd said, was to train blacks for their station in life: *'What is the use of teaching a Bantu child mathematics when it cannot use it in practice?'* Under the act all mission schools except Roman Catholic ones agreed to hand over control to the government, in return for receiving financial support. The ANC national executive wanted a permanent boycott of these black state schools. Although Mandela thought this unrealistic, the ANC called for children to stay away and tried to create schools of their own. But they were harassed by the police, parents became desperate, and the boycott had to be withdrawn.

Apartheid in schools became the norm, later to be followed by apartheid in universities, with the removal of the independence of Mandela's old academies, Fort Hare and Wits, and the imposition of strict racial segregation. Later on, in 1957—following reports of liaisons between blacks and whites—came the Immorality Act, outlawing sexual intercourse between whites and members of any other racial group. These interracial relationships repulsed apartheid purists and also embarrassed them, especially when Afrikaner men were involved, and still more when mixed-race children were born.

A black family friend of ours had been a clerk at the supreme court in Pretoria, where most of the major political trials took place. Then in 1959 the government decided that blacks should not carry out such "responsible tasks". He was replaced by a white man—whom he had to train for the job—and was then made redundant. Some apartheid laws were incongruous. Regulations reserving skilled jobs for whites to protect their privileged status allowed blacks to paint the undercoats on walls but prevented them from adding the final coats, a job that was reserved for white paint-ers. Similarly, blacks could hand bricks to white workers but not lay them.

By 1954 Verwoerd, now minister of Native Affairs, was pre-paring a much more ambitious scheme of "grand apartheid". He was convinced of the moral rightness of his plan to completely sep-arate blacks and whites, which could be achieved only by drastic social engineering and mass removals that had Stalinist echoes, though Verwoerd invoked Christianity in support of his eccentri-cally oppressive ideology. He was able to buy off many chieftains in rural areas, where chiefs were jealous of their territorial influence and privileges. Only a few, such as Albert Luthuli (with Mandela's support), were prepared to surrender their chieftainship rather than serve apartheid—as in wartime Europe, it required great courage not to collaborate with an all-powerful regime.

The next stage, the ANC leadership felt in 1953, was to broaden its vision for a democratic South Africa based upon social justice and human rights, and not just freedom from apartheid oppression. This was the genesis of the "Freedom Charter". The first stage would be for the ANC to convene a national conven-tion, called the "Congress of the People", representing all South Africans irrespective of race or color, to draw up a '*Freedom Charter for the Democratic South Africa of the Future*'. In the Congress Alliance the ANC was to be joined by the Indian Congress (formed by Mahatma Gandhi in 1894 while living in South Africa), the South African Congress of Trade Unions (SACTU), the newly formed Coloured Peoples' Organization and the Congress of Democrats

(COD), which had been formed mainly from ex-members of the Communist Party.

However, within the global context of an escalating "cold war", the charter was criticized in South Africa as '*a typical communist ploy*', using ANC leaders as gullible pawns. Actually, it was not directed against capitalists or Western democrats but against narrow nationalists, both "Africanists" in their movement and Afrikaners outside. Nevertheless, this was an example of how apartheid supporters would label almost any opponent, regardless of their beliefs or the evidence, as a '*communist fellow traveler*'—a charge frequently made at Mandela when he was nothing of the sort. Two years later, for instance, Mandela welcomed the opportunity that the charter would create for free enterprise to expand: '*For the first time in the history of this country, the non-European bourgeoisie will have the opportunity to own, in their own name and right, mills and factories, and trade and private enterprise will boom and flourish as never before*'.

We, the People of South Africa, declare for all our country and the world to know: that South Africa belongs to all who live in it, Black and White, and that no government can justly claim authority unless it is based on the will of all the people; that our people have been robbed of their birthright to land, liberty and peace by a form of government founded on injustice and inequality; that our country will never be prosperous or free until all our people live in brotherhood, enjoying equal rights and opportunities; that only a democratic state, based on the will of all the people, can secure to all their birthright without distinction of color, race, sex or belief; And therefore, we, the people of South Africa, Black and White together equals, countrymen and brothers adopt this Freedom Charter; And we pledge ourselves to strive together, sparing neither strength nor courage, until the democratic changes here set out have been won (FROM THE FREEDOM CHARTER, JUNE 1955).

The Congress of the People took place on June 25 and 26, 1954, on a private sports field in Kliptown, near Soweto, with three thousand delegates, mostly African, but hundreds of Indians, Coloureds and whites too. Like most of the organizers, Mandela was banned from the meeting, but he and Sisulu moved in disguise around the edge of the crowd, eluding the beady eyes of watching special branch officers. On the first day, the Freedom Charter was recited in three languages and approved with shouts of "Africa" by the crowd. On the second day, each section was acclaimed in turn, until the words "there shall be peace and friendship" were reached, when the meeting was suddenly disrupted by policemen with guns, bursting into the crowd and taking the name of everyone before they were allowed to leave—Mandela and Sisulu managing to get away.

Although it had been broken up, Mandela was elated with the outcome and said, '*The charter became a great beacon for the liberation struggle. . . . It captured the hopes and dreams of the people and acted as a blueprint for the future of the nation*'. The Freedom Charter opened with these words: '*We, the people of South Africa, declare for all our country and the world to know: That South Africa belongs to all who live in it, Black and White, and that no government can justly claim authority unless it is based on the will of the people*'. The charter was eventually endorsed at a special ANC conference in Orlando in April 1956, in the face of much dissention from self-styled "Africanists", who believed blacks should go it alone in the vanguard of the struggle and who were to split off two years later.

In August 1956, ten thousand women of all races gathered at the seat of government, the Union Buildings in Pretoria, in protest against the extension of the Pass Laws to women, and they left a petition with seven thousand signatures at the prime minister's office. Mandela was delighted with this show of strength and strongly supported separate initiatives by ANC women, though few were under any illusions that the government would listen.

The previous September (in 1955), his travel ban having expired, Mandela decided to take his first holiday for seven years to go home to the Transkei and visit his mother, family and friends from his youth. He was excited to see again his humble home and to eat the foods and soak in the rural atmosphere of his boyhood. He also had a political purpose, for the Transkei council of chiefs, the Bunga, had voted to accept the Bantu Authorities Act and become a so-called "homeland", ostensibly ruled by local African chiefs but with blacks separated off from whites into poor zones, complying with the fundamental architecture of apartheid and sup-plying a cheap migrant workforce for the city engines of the white economy.

In Mandela's homeland, his nephew and onetime hero at Fort Hare Kaiser Matanzima, was now paramount chief of Western Tembuland and had persuaded the Bunga to accept the act. Man-dela argued with him throughout the night, but there was deadlock—the two old allies were now opponents: Matanzima was allied with the ANC's enemies.

During his drive back through the Cape, Mandela stopped to confer with regional ANC leaders, before returning to Orlando, where he greeted his excited children with presents. '*Though not a true holiday, it had the same effect: I felt rejuvenated and ready to take up the fight once more*'.

But he had bleak news for the ANC's national leaders. The ANC's influence in the Transkei was waning, both because of the growing influence of leaders like Matanzima in the new structures of "Bantustan" governance and because of attacks by the security police. Here Mandela's combination of iron principle, pragmatism and political creativity, as well as his leadership courage, was revealed—a feature of his political personality that was to endure right through the next few decades and eventually on into power as the country's president. Because the ANC was being neutralized in "homeland" areas like the Transkei, he suggested it might participate in the new structures in order to maintain contact with the masses and as a platform for ANC ideas and policies to be spread.

His proposal was angrily rejected, however, and he ruefully reflected, '*In my early days, I, too, would have strenuously objected. But my sense of the country was that relatively few people were ready to make the sacrifices to join the struggle. We should meet the people on their own terms, even if that meant appearing to collaborate. My idea was that the movement should be a great tent that included as many people as possible*'.

In February 1956, Mandela made a brief trip to the Transkei with Sisulu to buy a plot of land near his birthplace, exhibiting again how, despite being a thoroughly sophisticated modern activist, his traditional upbringing still very much shaped his attitudes: '*I have always thought a man should own a house near the place he was born, where he might find a restfulness that eludes him elsewhere*'. More than forty years later in retirement, he was indeed to build a home and live there.

⁓

Soon after returning, and having enjoyed only several months of freedom since his last ban expired, he was banned for the third time, preventing him from leaving Johannesburg until 1961 and prohibiting him from going to meetings. This time his response was different. Instead of conforming as in the past, he was determined to circumvent the ban somehow: '*I was not going to let my involvement in the struggle and the scope of my political activities be determined by the enemy I was fighting against. I resolved not to become my own jailer*'.

However, the government had very different plans. He was

awakened early in the morning on December 5, 1956, by the police to search the house and arrest him for "high treason". Over the next ten days, another 155 leaders within the Congress of the People—mostly black but some white, Indian or Coloured, including virtually all the ANC leadership—were arrested on the same charge. The marathon trial that followed would cripple his political activity and law practice for the next five years.

The prisoners were all held in the Fort, the notorious prison on the hill overlooking Johannesburg, and for Mandela they were treated "*like animals*". The only compensation for the harsh conditions was that most prisoners had long been banned from meetings and travel and now had the first opportunity for a long time to exchange views with colleagues from other cities.

It would be ten months before the trial began. The prosecution argued that the accused conspired to overthrow the government by violence and replace it with a communist state, using evidence from the Defiance Campaign, the Sophiatown protests, and the Freedom Charter. For Mandela this was no ordinary trial. His comrades and he saw it for what it was: a '*political trial in which the government was persecuting us for taking actions that were morally justified*'.

A week after the treason arrests a bus boycott had begun in Alexandra—fourteen years after the one Mandela had taken part in when living there—and the government passed a bill requiring employers to subsidize the bus fare. That the boycott was successful at a time when leaders of the resistance were under arrest awaiting trial showed the depth of grassroots African anger. It was also the first piece of legislation to have been caused by African pressure since the Act of Union in 1910. The long trial brought the various racial groups even more closely together and effectively ensured cohesion in the resistance among them. The courtroom was often besieged by protesters, and when they returned home each evening, the accused were made to feel like heroes.

Meanwhile, Mandela's marriage to Evelyn had been deteriorating for some time as she became steadily alienated by his political activities, pleading that he return back to the Transkei with her. '*I patiently explained to her that politics was not a distraction but my life work, that it was an essential and fundamental part of my being*', he explained. And after his first arrest for treason in December 1956, he returned home on bail to find that she had moved out—though they were to remain on good terms.

However, Mandela's personal life soon changed for the better when he met Winnie Nomzamo Madikizela, a beautiful young social worker from the home area of Oliver Tambo, in the Transkei. She had come to Johannesburg in 1953 to study and in 1955 became the first black social worker at Baragwanath Hospital, in Soweto. She was sociable, spirited and fascinated by clothes (and by shoes, which she had never worn before she went to secondary school).

He had first noticed her waiting for a bus while driving by. By chance, within a few weeks she visited a law court with a friend, saw Mandela conducting a case, and soon afterward, in 1957, was introduced to him by Tambo's future wife, Adelaide. For Mandela it was love at first sight—and almost the moment he saw her he wanted to marry her. By now aged thirty-nine, magnetic and handsome, his friends were not sure what to make of the glamorous, innocent-looking twenty-two-year-old, who knew nothing of politics and seemed to belong to a different world. Winnie and Mandela spent as much time together as possible, between the treason trial and his law office.

They visibly fascinated each other, and after he had divorced Evelyn, they married in June 1958. He was given a relief from his bans to travel down to the Transkei for the wedding celebrations.

But his marriage to a young woman seventeen years his junior and the complications of his three alienated children did not provide the stable base that his friend Sisulu took for granted—with his wife Albertina his "backbone", sharing his political commitments. Winnie became only too aware how much politics dominated Mandela's life, and she soon developed her own political ambitions and instincts. She was drawn into the women's struggle and joined the Orlando branch of the ANC's Women's League, which earlier had organized a march of twenty thousand women to the Union Buildings in Pretoria to petition the prime minister against forcing women to carry passes. She was charged with inciting women not to carry passes and, four months after their marriage, joined a mass protest in Johannesburg, ignoring Mandela's efforts to dissuade her. He told her that, although he was proud of her political commitment, he was worried that if she lost her job, the one salary they could both depend upon would go, as his law firm had virtually collapsed under the combined weight of the treason trial and his political activities. In the event, Winnie, along with a thousand other women, was arrested and detained: '*He did not even pretend that I would have some special claim to his time. There never was any kind of life I can recall as family life, a young bride's life where you sit with your husband. You just couldn't tear Nelson from the people: the struggle, the nation came first*'.

The Treason Trial defense team included Bram Fischer, from an elite Afrikaner family, a communist who became a close friend of Mandela and a hero of the ANC. They had been embroiled for almost a year when, in December 1957, charges were suddenly dropped against some of the accused—but Mandela and the others were ordered to go on trial for treason in the Old Synagogue courtroom in the Afrikaner stronghold, Pretoria, with a new prosecutor, Oswald Pirow, an avowed Nazi supporter during the war.

Having opened on August 1, 1958, there were various legal stratagems and delays, and the trial did not resume until February 1959, where, at lunchtimes, many of the accused went outside for a meal provided in turn by the local Indian community and by sympathizers, including my anti-apartheid parents, where they first met and talked to Nelson Mandela (remembering him as '*a large, imposing, smiling man*').

The ANC's leaders' involvement day to day in the courtroom sucked up their energy and time; this was a godsend to their Africanist opponents who opposed the Freedom Charter and called for an end to cooperation with communists or other races. None of the Africanists were on trial; they moved freely around the country organizing and accusing ANC leaders of treating the membership like "voting cattle". The Africanists attacked Mandela and his allies for becoming closer to the whites, Indians and communists and distant from their own people.

In April 1958, the ANC had tried to mount a stay-at-home protest against the whites-only general election. The Africanists opposed this, and indeed it proved a fiasco. Their final break came in November that year, when the Africanists broke away from the ANC. Mandela saw the split as probably inevitable, and it was an ideological moment of truth for him and his remaining ANC comrades: they refused to sacrifice their multiracialism, whether in their policies or in the way they organized and cooperated with other racial groups.

In the middle of all this tension and high politics, Winnie bore them a daughter, Zeni, and later, in September 1958, there was an ominous shift at the top of the government. Having taken over from Prime Minister Malan in 1954, J. G. Strijdom died and was succeeded by the apartheid fundamentalist Dr. Hendrik Verwoerd, who began to lead an even more ruthless new government.

In April 1959, the Africanists formed their own party, the Pan Africanist Congress (PAC), expressly opposed to the ANC's multiracialism. Echoing some of the sentiments that had prompted Mandela and others to form the Youth League fifteen years earlier, PAC members considered the ANC insufficiently militant, and they believed whites and Indians were foreign minorities: South Africa should be for Africans alone. Their leader, Robert Sobukwe, was welcomed by conservatives in Europe and America as a promising alternative to the ANC—an example of the Cold War prism through which the freedom struggle was viewed by the West. Although by now most ANC leaders were either on trial or banned, the formation of the PAC spurred the ANC to be more militant and it carried out some successful economic boycotts.

Early in 1960, the newly elected British prime minister, Harold Macmillan, unexpectedly and memorably spoke about a "Wind of Change" blowing through Africa as the British at last began to catch up with the tide of anticolonialism then sweeping in. His speech, delivered to the South African Parliament in February that year, shocked the Verwoerd government and delighted Mandela, who thought it "terrific".

The ANC had meanwhile come under pressure to defy the Pass Laws with a burning of pass books campaign, and at the December 1959 annual congress the national executive reported that '*the struggle for the repeal of the Pass Laws has begun*'. Mandela, Sisulu, and Tambo helped to prepare a plan, first for the extension of the economic boycott campaign and then for an antipass campaign, to culminate in a bonfire of passes on ANC Freedom Day, June 26.

The PAC, however, beat them to it, and on March 21, 1960, Sobukwe and about 150 others went without passes to Orlando police station. In Cape Town about fifteen hundred did the same, and huge crowds gathered in protest. In the small township of Sharpeville, an hour's drive south of Johannesburg, about ten thousand people surrounded the police station fence. Although unarmed and peaceful, the sheer size of the crowd unnerved the policemen, who suddenly opened fire, killing sixty-seven and

Sharpeville, March 23, 1960, peaceful protest becomes carnage: people fleeing in terror as White police gun down the crowd. Image ID: EC7M78.

wounding three hundred, including women and children. Most were shot in the back as they turned and ran away in panic. It was a horrific event, and pictures of what became known as the Sharpeville Massacre reverberated round the world. The US State Department blamed the government for the massacre, as for the first time did the UN Security Council (though with Britain and France abstaining). The South African stock market collapsed, and there were reports of whites preparing to emigrate.

The massacre had transformed the black political scene and gave the PAC a huge boost. Mandela spent the whole night with Sisulu, Joe Slovo and others, planning how to respond. They decided that ANC leaders, beginning with Luthuli, should publicly burn their pass books. On March 26, Luthuli was photographed holding the charred remains of his book. Mandela did the same, and a few hundred others followed their example. Two days later the vast majority of black workers obeyed the ANC's call for a stay-at-home, and the commissioner of police suspended arrests for not carrying passes. For ten days after Sharpeville the whole apartheid edifice seemed to be shaking.

Anticipating a fierce response from the state, including the likely banning of their organization, Mandela and the ANC leaders decided that Oliver Tambo should go overseas to represent it and establish a broad ANC base in exile. He slipped out illegally and soon set up an office in newly independent Ghana. Over the next thirty years, Tambo's international statesmanship and the bond of trust between him and Mandela in jail were central to the ANC's survival—Tambo being the undersung hero of the struggle.

By March 30, a general strike had paralyzed Cape Town, which was the PAC's stronghold. When the police began brutally attacking the townships, some thirty thousand black workers marched into the city. The same day the government declared a state of emergency with martial law powers to crack down on any dissent. More than two thousand people were detained. In the early hours, Mandela's house was raided and turned upside down. He was taken to join fifty other detainees in jail, where he spent the night herded into a small cell, with no beds, blankets or food and with a hole in the floor that served as a toilet. After several days, and enduring these stinking conditions, Mandela was taken with fellow accused to resumed hearings of the Treason Trial but was incarcerated again overnight after each day in court.

The government backed up this attack on April 8, 1960, by introducing legislation that made the ANC and the PAC illegal. For Mandela and his colleagues, membership of the ANC and even furthering its aims had immediately become a crime with a prison sentence certain. '*The struggle had entered a new phase. We were now outlaws*', he reflected.

The next day, to add to the sense of turmoil in the country, Prime Minister Verwoerd was shot and wounded at an agricultural show in Johannesburg—but not by a black activist; instead, perversely, by a deranged white farmer. He recovered rapidly and took charge again; thereafter, the police enforced their powers even more brutally. People could not draw a pension or post office savings without a pass, and they began queuing up to replace the passes they had burned. A month after Sharpeville, apartheid was firmly back in the saddle, and the resistance was being remorselessly crushed.

Mandela and his fellow Treason Trial defendants were by now finding it impossible to properly conduct their defense, because they were prisoners living in dreadful conditions and the restrictions imposed by the state of emergency were draconian. Prison regulations even banned meetings necessary for the defendants between black and white, or male and female. So they unanimously agreed that the defense lawyers should withdraw from the case in protest and the defendants should conduct their own defense—the shocked court so informed on April 26. There were obvious risks but also some advantages as Mandela was '*angry and eager to take on the state*'.

During these months, the court became a platform for ANC leaders to enunciate their views in public—an opportunity they relished because most had been silenced through bannings, in

Mandela's case for three years. He gave evidence on August 3, reaffirming the ANC's historic commitment to nonviolence and explaining that, while he was not a communist, the ANC had received great support from communists and he would not apologize for working with them.

At the end of August 1960, the state of emergency was lifted and most of the other prisoners were released. Immediately the ANC set up an emergency committee. But with some two thousand people including leading ANC figures detained, it was severely restricted in what it could deliver. So the ANC decided to carry on underground with some of its key activists working away while in hiding. For those doing so, *"politics"*, Mandela said, '*went from being a risky occupation to a truly perilous one*'. There could not have been clearer evidence of the way the apartheid state, by denying the ANC elementary democratic rights, forced Mandela and his comrades down a road that would eventually include armed struggle. For the detainees, the end of the emergency was a real fillip.

They left prison to a jubilant reception from comrades and relatives. Mandela was ecstatically reunited with his young child and wife Winnie, whom he hugged and kissed. They then slept in their own bed for the first time in five months.

But his joy was short-lived, for the Treason Trial was to continue for another energy- and commitment-sapping nine months. By late 1960, Mandela's previously successful and wide-ranging life in Johannesburg was rapidly coming to an end—his law practice had collapsed, many friends were in exile, his social network in Orlando had gone, and financially he was ruined. His life with Winnie was constantly interrupted with political tasks, and when she had their second daughter Zindzi in December, he arrived at the hospital too late to be with her. His political life was already half underground.

With the Treason Trial still in session, Mandela and Sisulu moved around illicitly all over the country to organize an "All-in Conference", as it was to be called, to be held in the Natal town of

Pietermaritzburg in March 1961. There were 1,400 delegates from 150 different groups, the ANC dominating, with Mandela secretly scheduled to speak because the ban preventing him speaking publicly had just expired. At a meeting the day before he was due to leave for the All-in Conference, the ANC emergency committee met in secret and decided that Mandela must go underground. They knew that, even if acquitted in the Treason Trial, he and his colleagues would likely be rearrested or banned again or both. Sisulu was convinced that the ANC must have a single leader underground and that it must be Mandela, as chief spokesman for his people.

That night he told Winnie, '*It was as though [she] could read my thoughts. . . . She knew I was about to embark on a life that neither of us wanted*'. Ready for the trial verdict, she packed him a small suitcase, its destination still uncertain: to go with him either to prison or on the run underground.

Seeing Mandela there addressing them in public at the conference for the first time since 1952, the audience erupted with excitement as he strode onto the platform, their charismatic leader at last before them. They rousingly shouted the new ANC slogan "Amandla! Ngawethu!" (power to the people) when he appealed again for African unity, and the conference called on the government to summon a national convention. If this was refused, the ANC would organize a multiracial, three-day, stay-at-home protest (strikes were illegal, stay-at-homes were not), beginning on May 31, the day that South Africa was to become a republic after a whites-only referendum the previous October. Mandela was to be chief organizer of this event. Then he disappeared from the hall, which was riddled with security police informers, as suddenly as he had appeared. He would not be seen on a public platform again in South Africa for fully twenty-nine years.

He returned to Pretoria for the Treason Trial and, on March 29, 1961, it was announced that a unanimous verdict of "not guilty" had been reached. The court decided that the prosecution had not proven their case that the ANC was a communist organi-zation or that the Freedom Charter was a communist manifesto. Crowds of supporters jostling outside were overjoyed, cheering the defendants. But Mandela had no illusions. As later transpired, a deeply embarrassed government simply decided to be even more brutal, both in its repressive legislation and in its security police operations.

Afterward Mandela did not return home but instead disap-peared: *'Although others were in a festive mood and eager to celebrate, I knew the authorities could strike at any moment'*.

—

Mandela went around the country for two months, going to ANC leadership meetings at all levels and popping up everywhere to talk to white newspaper editors. This produced countrywide news reports dubbing him "the Black Pimpernel" as he eluded police road blocks with a warrant out for his arrest. He was often disguised as a chauffeur, a chef, or a "garden boy", finding the role of chauf-feur (neat peaked cap included) ideal because it enabled him to drive around freely as black men often did in their white masters' cars.

However, it was not an easy life, as he described: *'Living under-ground requires a seismic psychological shift. One has to plan every action, however small and seemingly insignificant. Nothing is innocent. Everything is questioned . . . I became a creature of the night'*. Based in Johannes-burg, he would move around as required, hiding in the day in empty flats or safe houses where he could be on his own. Although he desperately missed Winnie and their young children, there was one compensation: *'I welcomed the opportunity to be by myself—to plan, to think, to plot'*.

He voraciously read books on war, from Clausewitz's *On War* to Reitz's classic *Commando*, about the Boer War. But it was the Cuban Revolution in 1959 that most inspired him.

South Africa said goodbye to the Commonwealth and voted in a republic on May 31, 1961, while Mandela crossed the nation organizing a stay-at-home protest for the Republic Day celebrations. Early that morning, tanks patrolled the townships with helicopters overhead. To the ANC's fury, the PAC was calling on everyone to go to work as it objected to cooperating with other races. The English-language press and radio conspired with the government—publishing every warning against the ANC beforehand and playing down its successes on the day. In hiding and unable to watch events themselves, Mandela and the action committee were forced to judge the success of the protest from press headlines. They called it off after the first day; it fizzled out amid intimidation and massive police raids (some ten thousand blacks were detained). The last disciplined, mass nonviolent demonstration to be held in South Africa was over.

Mandela was now convinced that peaceful protests had reached a dead end, and in fact he had been discussing abandoning nonviolence for more than a year. He had always been more rejecting of nonviolence than were Sisulu or Tambo, but now ordinary people were overtaking him with an impatience that he felt could not be ignored. In the Cape, the PAC soon produced an armed offshoot called Poqo ("Alone"), which assassinated whites in reprisal for brutal oppression, and a group of white Liberals and others organized the African Resistance Movement (ARM), which planned sabotage on government installations.

A month after Republic Day, Mandela proposed that the ANC should form its own military wing, with autonomous leadership separate from the ANC though responsible to it. A meeting with its Indian, Coloured and white allies confirmed the formation of a new military organization under Mandela, to be called Umkhonto we Sizwe (MK; Spear of the nation), which was to be quite distinct from the ANC.

Mandela threw himself into his new role with enthusiasm. In a statement from hiding on ANC Freedom Day, June 26, 1961, he announced, '*We plan to make government impossible*'. With a warrant out for his arrest, he was now hunted everywhere and in October found a new hiding place at Liliesleaf Farm, an isolated house with some outbuildings in Rivonia outside Johannesburg; Liliesleaf was secretly owned by the Communist Party. Initially, Mandela had moved in as a "houseboy" to look after the place, using an alias and wearing the standard dark blue overalls of a black male servant. He frequently left in the evenings in disguise, to meet ANC leaders and others, and Winnie visited him there with their two little girls, careful with her journey as she switched cars to and fro during the trips. Based in hiding there, he continued to travel throughout South Africa.

On December 16, 1961 (Dingaan's Day, which commemorated the Afrikaner massacre of a Zulu army in 1838), as directed by Mandela, MK carried out its first acts of sabotage, with explosions in Johannesburg, Port Elizabeth and Durban. These took the country by surprise, receiving huge media attention, spreading fear among whites, and indicating to blacks that the ANC now had the power and intention to strike at the heart of the white state. To coincide with the attacks, thousands of leaflets were distributed across the land, stating that MK had been formed and why. MK's campaign of placing incendiary bombs in government offices, post offices and electrical substations involved two hundred attacks in the following eighteen months expressly aimed at state installations, not at people.

Mandela with others in MK had considered this strategy carefully before deciding on attacks against state facilities, assessing in turn sabotage, guerrilla warfare, open revolution and terrorism.

The last was out of the question and only sabotage was a practical proposition, given MK's very limited resources and infancy. As Mandela explained,

Our strategy was to make selective forays against military installations, power plants, telephone lines and transportation links; targets that would not only hamper the military effectiveness of the state, but also frighten National

Party supporters, scare away foreign capital and weaken the economy. This we hoped would bring the government to the bargaining table. Strict instructions were given to members of MK that we would countenance no loss of life.

Soon after the first explosions, MK—under its commander in chief Mandela—started thinking about guerrilla warfare, and it arranged for key leaders to go abroad for training in China and elsewhere, followed by volunteers.

In December 1961, the ANC president Albert Luthuli accepted the Nobel Peace Prize, a huge international endorsement of the ANC's struggle and a sign of its growing worldwide impact.

Money and military training were sought from newly independent African nations, and early in 1962, Mandela secretly left the country to meet their governments and to speak at an African summit meeting to explain the ANC's plans. On January 10, 1962, he crossed the Tanzanian border, staying overnight in a local hotel where he was immediately struck by the multiracial atmosphere, with blacks and whites mixing freely and talking happily: '*Never before had I been in a public place or hotel where there was no color bar. . . . I then truly realized that I was in a country ruled by Africans*'. Tanzania had recently become independent, and Mandela was delighted by the modest, man-of-the-people style of its new president, Julius Nyerere.

Mandela flew on to Ghana, met up with Oliver Tambo, and was struck at how Tambo had quickly become an impressive ambassador for the ANC, with burgeoning international contacts. Later in Ethiopia, Mandela was able to meet some of the ANC guerrilla volunteers: '*It was a proud moment, for these men had volunteered for duty in an army I was then attempting to create. . . . It was the first time I was ever saluted by my own soldiers*'.

At the pan-African conference, Mandela met the Ethiopian

emperor Haile Selassie and gave the most important speech he had ever made, warning that the situation in South Africa was "explosive". He explained the background to the freedom struggle, how nonviolence had been crushed, and why an armed campaign was the only alternative. Despite obtaining pledges of assistance, there was still some reluctance by African governments to support violent struggles elsewhere on the continent, with their new leaders still worried about the ANC's cooperation with white communists, a concern he was to hear repeatedly and that explained the PAC's foothold with these African leaders.

> *In Africa, as our contribution to peace, we are resolved to end such evils as oppression, White supremacy and racial discrimination, which are incompatible with world peace and security.* (from Albert Luthuli's acceptance speech on receiving the Nobel Peace Prize, Oslo, Norway, December 10, 1961)

> *I am also here today as representative of the millions of people across the globe, the anti-apartheid movement, the governments and organizations that joined with us, not to fight against South Africa as a country or any of its peoples, but to oppose an inhuman system and sue for a speedy end to the apartheid crime against humanity.*
> *These countless human beings, both inside and outside our country, had the nobility of*

spirit to stand in the path of tyranny and injustice, without seeking selfish gain. They recognized that an injury to one is an injury to all and therefore acted in defense of justice and a common human decency.

Because of their courage and persistence for many years, we can, today, even set the dates when all humanity will join together to celebrate one of the outstanding victories of our century.

When that moment comes, we shall, together, rejoice in a common victory over racism, apartheid and White minority rule. (FROM NELSON MANDELA'S ACCEPTANCE SPEECH ON RECEIVING THE NOBEL PEACE PRIZE, OSLO, NORWAY, DECEMBER 10, 1993)

Mandela found that the PAC, which also had a speaker there, had been spreading malicious stories against the ANC in the African states, calling it a "*Xhosa army*" and "*riddled with White communists*". He realised that the ANC's alliance with whites and Indians did not go down well with the black nationalism of the rest of Africa, and he found it hard to justify the ANC's multiracialism to African leaders. The rest of his African tour included Morocco. While there he spent time with Algerian fighters, and after talking to Algeria's military commander, he realised there was no question of trying to overthrow the apartheid regime; it had to be forced to the negotiating table.

Mandela went on with flying visits to the new black states of West Africa, and then to London, where Tambo had already been shunned by the Foreign Office as it paid more attention to the PAC and was worried by the ANC's communist links. There Mandela met the editor of the influential *Observer*, David Astor, and persuaded him to switch sympathy from the PAC to the ANC; he also held talks with the Labour and Liberal leaders Hugh Gaitskell and Jo Grimond. When asked why he was going back, Mandela said, '*A leader stays with his people*'. On the way home he stopped off in Ethiopia, in June, for a six-month military course to prepare him as MK leader. He was taught to shoot and instructed in demolition, mortars, small bombs and mines: '*I found myself being molded into a soldier and began to think as a soldier thinks—a far cry from the way a politician thinks*'.

—

Back home the government was determined to track down Mandela and searched or visited Winnie at home regularly. In July, the Sabotage Bill was passed, carrying the death penalty for quite minor acts of destruction. Headquartered in Rivonia, MK members were pushing ahead with plans for bolder action, and they urgently needed Mandela back to resume command.

He arrived at Rivonia on July 24 and was reunited with Winnie and their two girls the next day. That evening at a crucial strategy discussion with Sisulu and other key ANC leaders, Mandela reported on the distrust he had encountered and concluded that their friends must understand that '*it is the ANC that is to pilot the struggle*'. He proposed that the Congress Alliance should remain as formed except with the ANC as the clear leader, particularly on African affairs. In the circumstances of proven success through a multiracial alliance of equal partnership with Indians, Coloureds and white communists, it did not surprise Mandela that they received his recommendation unhappily. But as a leader he had never shirked tough choices.

Next he left for Durban to report to his president, Albert Luthuli, who was also unhappy about seemingly being dictated to by outsiders in Africa. But Mandela insisted to him that the plan '*was simply to effect essentially cosmetic changes in order to make the ANC more intelligible—and more palatable to our allies'*. He visited others in the Durban area and then went back to a safe house to meet the MK regional command. The next afternoon, on August 5, 1962, dressed in his white chauffeur's coat and with the white car owner in the back, he set off back to Johannesburg, feeling good as he viewed the attractive Natal countryside passing by.

But it was to be a fateful trip. Soon after passing the town of Howick, he noticed a car full of white men rush past and, looking in his mirror, noticed two more similar cars behind. '*I knew in that instant that my life on the run was over*', he recalled as the police flagged him down. They brusquely brushed aside his attempted alias. '*You're Nelson Mandela*', they insisted, arresting him after seventeen months on the run. The police had obviously been tipped off by an informer, many of whom had infiltrated the movement. Although he knew this could have happened at any time, as his clandestine life was precarious and dependent upon the trust of so many, Mandela was devastated.

He was driven to Johannesburg and charged with incitement to strike and leaving the country without a passport; he was relieved that there was clearly no evidence to bring much more serious charges to link him with MK. Familiar to the sitting magistrate as a practicing attorney-at-law in the court over the years, he was treated with courtesy as a fellow professional. As an experienced lawyer, he had taken the decision to defend himself, deciding that this would best enable him to '*use [his] trial as a showcase for the ANC's moral opposition to racism*'. As he left the court to be escorted back to prison, he was cheered by hundreds of supporters chanting ANC slogans. With several months to wait for the full hearing, he began studying by correspondence for a law degree at London University. Winnie was permitted to visit him regularly with clean clothes and tasty food. Although Mandela felt her deep love and devotion, he was sharply aware how difficult it was for her, particularly with two small girls back in their house. The trial was shifted to Pretoria just before it was due to begin, and Sisulu meanwhile disappeared to go underground and continue to plot sabotage.

Instead of his usual suit and tie, Mandela appeared on the first day—October 22, 1962—in a traditional Xhosa leopard-skin kaross to symbolize that he '*was a Black man in a White man's court*'. The courtroom, in Pretoria's Old Synagogue, was surrounded by police and packed with Africans including Winnie, also in traditional African dress. Mandela walked in, raised his fist to the Black public gallery and shouted "Amandla" (power), which received a loud response of "Ingawethu" (the power is ours!). My mother, Adelaine, attended to monitor the trial for the Liberal Party magazine *Contact* and, often the only person in the public gallery reserved for whites, Mandela would turn to her and give a clenched-fist salute, which she returned.

Winnie Mandela attended the trial each day, often looking magnificent in traditional dress. Once my two small sisters went with my mother, and Winnie bent down and kissed the little blonde girls, to the evident outrage of the onlooking white policemen, who thought such interracial affection quite beyond the pale. Mandela's traditional attire had also offended the local police colonel, who demanded he hand it over. But he refused, saying he would appeal its removal right up to the supreme court if it were confiscated. It wasn't—illustrating that, even under the weight of a brutal police state, which trampled all over the rule of law, some legal avenues could still be pursued.

Mandela was confronted with more than a hundred witnesses whose evidence demonstrated he had left the country unlawfully and had, during the May 1961 stay-at-home campaign, incited black workers to strike.

Knowing that he had no defense because he had committed these offenses, Mandela confounded the prosecution by refusing to call any witnesses or give evidence himself and instead delivered an hour-long statement in mitigation. He described how African grievances had been repeatedly thwarted despite peaceful protests and representations over the decades and that government violence had left the ANC with no option but to respond in kind. Whatever sentence awaited him, Mandela concluded, would not alter his commitment to pursue the struggle.

On November 7, 1962, the magistrate jailed him for five years with no parole. As he was taken away to Pretoria prison, Mandela raised a clenched fist, shouting Amandla! to which the packed gallery responded by singing their national anthem, "Nkosi Sikelel' iAfrika." In detention, he was stripped, his kaross was confiscated and he was given the normal prison outfit for black men: short trousers. But the authorities were again taking on more than they had bargained for. Mandela refused the attire, saying there was no way he would be humiliated into wearing shorts and that he would appeal to a court if necessary.

This demeaning of black prisoners, as if they were boys not men, had echoes of the manner in which the term "boy" was patronizingly applied by whites to all black men in daily civilian life. From an early age, I remember castigating friends when they called out to their gardeners in this way. The spectacle of bumptious young whites casually talking down to graying black grandfathers epitomized for me the daily indignity of apartheid that prisoner Mandela was subjected to.

Mandela also refused the terrible prison food, insisting he would only eat food brought in by friends. The authorities responded by enabling him to wear long trousers and receive outside food but at the price of isolating him on his own from other political prisoners.

This he found pretty unbearable: without a wristwatch, a book or a writing pad, and with the cell light on all day and night, '*every hour seemed like a year*' to him. After several weeks, he swapped his long trousers for the company of his fellow "politicals" and accepted the invariably cold and tasteless prison food.

He had been especially keen to talk to Robert Sobukwe, the PAC leader, who had been in jail since Sharpeville and who gave him a warm welcome. Their dialogue was proceeding positively until the authorities became suspicious and ensured they were always kept apart, even during courtyard exercises or sewing filthy mailbags. But after six months, in May 1963, Mandela was given ten minutes' notice before being driven overnight in a van with no windows and only a latrine bucket on the thousand-mile (1,600 km) journey to Robben Island, South Africa's equivalent to Alcatraz, eight miles (13.5 km) from the Cape Town mainland. On arrival, he was met by white warders shouting in Afrikaans: '*This is the island. Here you will die*'.

· 5 ·

Prisoner

To reach Robben Island, Mandela and three fellow prisoners had been chained together and forced to stand in the bowels of an old ship, which rocked in the heavy Cape rollers, as warders urinated down on them through their only channel for air and daylight, a single porthole to the deck.

The island, its reputation cold, inhospitable and oppressive in the apartheid times, had after Sharpeville been established as a prison to hold waves of political prisoners as well as common criminals. During the rising political agitation from 1962, it had come under a brutal regime for political prisoners, with savage assaults by the white warders common.

Humiliation was constant. On arrival, Mandela was herded unceremoniously with other prisoners into a room, the floor covered with water ankle deep, and ordered to undress. Their garments were quickly searched and thrown into the water, whereupon they were ordered to dress again in soaking clothes and served cold porridge before being herded into a large cell to sleep.

It was a harsh regime, pounding stones in the heat during the day and subject to constant harassment and intimidation by white warders determined to break their spirit. Mandela, however, had a certain aura about him, and he was quick to promise court action if attacked or threatened. The regime had never come across any prisoner like him before, confident as a lawyer in his rights, oblivious to their petty humiliations and almost imperious in his disdain, though always courteous and respectful if treated accordingly.

Robben Island, c.1990–2002. Aerial view of Robben Island, with the city of Cape Town and Table Mountain in the background. Image ID: AP8NP8.

However, he was tormented by learning through the news blackout that his wife Winnie had been issued with a banning order in January 1963. Although Mandela was able to stand up for himself on Robben Island, he could not protect his wife outside. He felt a total failure as a husband, suffering terrible nightmares and waking in cold sweats. What worried him almost more than anything was that Winnie, though courageous, had a headstrong, reckless nature, and he feared that the special branch would trap her into confrontation. Vivacious and dignified, she continued to work in a child welfare office, caring for their two little daughters, Zeni and Zindzi, unable to communicate with or visit her husband, and being harassed by the police who accused her of violating her banning orders.

That May, the government had produced its most drastic security legislation, which included the notorious Ninety-Day Law, enabling the police to hold anyone for three months incommunicado without trial. Arrests of key members of the resistance quickly followed. These new powers also came in handy when, on July 11, 1963, a band of armed police with dogs raided Liliesleaf Farm in Rivonia and arrested some of Mandela's closest friends, including the leading ANC and Umkhonto we Sizwe (MK) figures Walter Sisulu, Govan Mbeki and Ahmed Kathrada. They collected hundreds of documents, including an ambitious and highly sensitive plan called "Operation Mayibuye", which proposed establishing guerrilla groups throughout South Africa, to be eventually supported by an armed invasion including foreign troops landed by submarine and aircraft. It was an adventurist and unrealistic scheme about which Sisulu and others had strong reservations. Mandela had not been in Rivonia since the previous year so could not have authorized Mayibuye. But there were many documents discovered in his own handwriting, and he ruefully observed, '*In one fell swoop, the police had captured the entire high command of Umkhonto we Sizwe. The raid was a coup for the state*'.

Initially oblivious to the Rivonia arrests, Mandela was suddenly transported off the island in June 1963 to retrace the long journey to Pretoria Local Prison, the government claiming it was for '*his own protection*', albeit against nonexistent threats from Pan Africanist Congress (PAC) prisoners. Although placed in solitary confinement, he nevertheless managed to communicate with other comrades in the prison, gradually discovering to his alarm that they included some captured after undergoing military training outside South Africa. Then another shock: he spotted the foreman from Liliesleaf Farm and instantly realised that their underground base—Rivonia—must have been discovered.

They were all charged under the 1962 Sabotage Act, which turned the normal presumption of innocence until proven guilty on its head and required the defendants to prove their innocence. It also carried the death penalty. Ominously, their lawyers, led by

Bram Fischer, warned that death sentences were quite possible amid the lurid newspaper headlines and ugly climate then prevailing. Mandela as the First Accused knew he was most vulnerable: '*From that moment on, we lived in the shadow of the gallows*'.

What became known as the Rivonia trial opened in the supreme court in Pretoria in October 1963. The inside was packed with local and international journalists, while the outside was ringed by armed police and a huge crowd chanting and singing, which buoyed the prisoners. Entering the court, Mandela led his fellow accused in raising a clenched-fist salute to the packed visitors gallery, which responded with the by-now-familiar ANC chants: Amandla! Ngawethu! Mayibuye Afrika! The police quickly noted the names of all the spectators doing so.

The infamous prosecutor Percy Yutar had, however, botched the first indictment, which even alleged that Mandela had committed acts of sabotage at times when he was actually in prison. After a powerful attack from Bram Fischer, the judge quashed it and the full trial began only on December 3, 1963. The prosecution produced some 250 documents from Liliesleaf including, much to Mandela's chagrin, his false passport and all his books and notes, which he had secretly asked be removed before the Rivonia arrests; apparently his comrades had decided these might have some historic value.

Yutar in his opening statement painted a lurid picture of thousands of ubiquitous ANC guerrillas supported by foreign armed units planning terror and insurrection across the country to bring '*chaos, disorder and turmoil*' and smash white civilization. But under rhetoric calculated to create an atmosphere where the defendants became complete ogres, there was plenty of hard evidence to secure convictions. The star prosecution witness turned out to be Bruno Mtolo, a saboteur and member of the Communist Party. He had been at the meeting in Durban shortly before the police were tipped off about Mandela's final car journey as a chauffeur on the run. Mtolo had also visited Rivonia. Granted immunity, he was used to demonstrate the prosecution's case that both the ANC and

MK had to all intents and purposes been dissolved into the Communist Party, coming under its direct control in a mission to spread violence and subversion. This was a travesty—the ANC's express exclusion of any life- or injury-threatening action totally ignored. Additionally, much of his evidence was fabricated. But it served the state's purpose, prompting Mandela to decide that he might be better to give a statement from the dock rather than be subject to cross-examination under which he could incriminate himself further.

Amid all this pressure and tension, his life hanging on the whim of the court, he pined after Winnie. Unlike other relatives of the accused who were able to attend the court, her banning order prevented this. So she appealed personally to the prime minister, who finally relented—but with a firm qualification that this permission would immediately be withdrawn if she misbehaved or caused others to do so, or if she wore the traditional African dress that had so offended the authorities in the Synagogue trial the previous year. Mandela was thrilled to spot her sitting in the gallery, petite in her European clothing, and to touch her and hear of family news during court recesses, though as two banned people under surveillance they could not communicate anything political.

Mandela had spent two weeks preparing what would become a four-hour statement, and Bram Fischer opened the case for the defense on April 20. A murmur swept through the court as he conceded that some of the prosecution's evidence would not be disputed, but he insisted that its major thrust would be rejected, and strongly so. In particular, he challenged their assumption that the ANC and MK were seamlessly one organization—its political and military wings—when they were constituted entirely separately and also that they were mere fronts for the Communist Party.

Then came the supreme moment of the trial—when Fischer called Accused Number One. The prosecutor, Yutar, was very concerned about both Mandela's powerful presence and the normal court rules preventing interruption or cross-examination of a statement from the dock. Mandela rose, aware of Winnie watching as well as his mother, who had journeyed up from the Transkei.

The whole court hushed in anticipation. Here was his platform to explain and justify his leadership as a freedom fighter for his people. It was to become a historic statement—and his last public words for nearly twenty-seven years.

During his address, which lasted fully four hours and held the court spellbound, Mandela did not deny his actions, the planning of sabotage or the strategy of resistance. On the contrary, he proclaimed these as the only alternative available to them given the state's merciless crushing of all legal and peaceful opposition.

He ended with the words that would capture headlines the next day and capture the imagination of people for decades to come:

During my lifetime I have dedicated myself to this struggle of the African people. I have fought against White domination, and I have fought against Black domination. I have cherished the ideal of a democratic and free society in which all persons live together in harmony and with equal opportunities. It is an ideal which I hope to live for and achieve. But if needs be, it is an ideal for which I am prepared to die.

Bram Fischer had pleaded with him not to end with this, arguing it would condemn him to hang. But as on so many other occasions in his momentous life, Mandela was resolute. All his instincts told him this must be said, regardless. The speech identified him clearly as the leader, not only of the ANC but also of the whole opposition to apartheid, and it reverberated around the world as a manifesto for anti-apartheid campaigners everywhere.

The remaining accused then faced an appearance in the dock, with cross-examination, beginning with Sisulu, who had a knack of asking a simple question and demanding an answer, and so survived intact five full days of relentless questioning. Indeed, all Mandela's comrades acquitted themselves well, and after the defense case had ended, the judge adjourned for three weeks to consider his verdict.

When the court reassembled on June 11, 1964, the accused were found guilty of sabotage; the verdict was what Mandela and the others had prepared themselves for. They had stood proud in the dock as freedom fighters. Now they awaited their fate the next morning, the judge inviting any submissions before delivering sentences. Mandela was prepared for the death penalty: '*To be truly prepared for something, one must actually expect it. . . . We were all prepared, not because we were brave but because we were realistic. I thought of a line from Shakespeare: "Be absolute for death; for either death or life will be the sweeter"*'.

That night, after consulting as best they could, Mandela, Sisulu and Mbeki decided that they would not appeal for mercy, nor would they subsequently appeal against whatever sentence awaited them. Their lawyers were distraught. But to do otherwise, the accused decided, would contradict the moral basis for the defense and contaminate the future struggles.

The trial had become a focus for international pressure. The United Nations called for their unconditional release and for that of all political prisoners in South Africa. Dockworkers threatened not to handle South African trade. Heads of government, British Labour MPs and US congressmen pleaded for clemency. Although Prime Minister Hendrik Verwoerd later boasted that none of this had any influence, it did create a context for Judge Quartus de Wet's final decision. He listened first to mitigation pleas from the defense, supported by Alan Paton, renowned author of *Cry the Beloved Country* and president of the South African Liberal Party, who did not support violence but stated the defendants had only the choice to '*bow their heads and submit, or resist by force*'. If they did not receive clemency, he added, South Africa's future would be dark indeed.

> *Today when I look at Robben Island I see it as a celebration of the struggle and a symbol of the finest qualities of the human spirit, rather than as a monument to the brutal tyranny and oppression of apartheid.*
>
> *Robben Island is a place where courage endured in the face of endless hardship, a place where people kept on believing when it seemed their dreams were hopeless and a place where wisdom and determination overcame fear and human frailty. It is true that Robben Island was once a place of darkness, but out of that darkness has come a wonderful brightness, a light so powerful that it could not be hidden behind prison walls, held back by prison bars or hemmed in by the surrounding sea.*

Winter was closing in on Friday, June 12, 1964, when Mandela and the others, tense, though prepared for the worst, were shepherded into the dock to learn their fate. Summoned to stand, they noticed the judge was nervous and glanced at each other expecting this indicated the gallows. But he appeared to accept part of the defense case that the ANC was not itself a guerrilla organization like MK, nor was it a communist front: '*I have decided not to impose the supreme penalty, which in a case like this would usually be the proper penalty for the crime, but consistent with my duty that is the only leniency I can show. The sentence in the case of all the accused will be one of life imprisonment*'.

It was a dramatic moment. Mandela, though resigned to imprisonment, was elated that he would after all live to fight another day. As the eight guilty prisoners were taken away, they could hear ANC chants and songs from the jubilant crowd outside, and that night in Pretoria Local Prison they all joined in with freedom songs and chants with fellow prisoners.

After a few days in Pretoria Local, on June 12, 1964, Mandela, Sisulu, and five other ANC leaders were suddenly taken from their cells in the early hours of the morning and flown in a small plane to Robben Island. They landed on an airstrip, the bleak winter wind blowing through their khaki prison garments, to be greeted by grim guards armed with automatic guns.

By now Mandela was aged forty-five and facing the rest of his life in a cell so tiny—less than ten feet (three meters) by just six feet (two meters)—that both his head and feet bumped up against the walls as he lay in his bed. It was to be his home for the next eighteen years. There was a small barred window through which the wind would blow, freezing in winter, with just three thin blankets and a straw floor mat.

—

The ANC's entire leadership had been sliced off, and the scope for internal resistance was paper thin. That same year, another draconian piece of legislation removed the right that some blacks had to reside in urban areas, and it empowered the government to "endorse out" any black if it deemed the black person to be "undesirable" or "idle."

A month later, in July 1964, a group of white members of the ARM (African Resistance Movement), including close family friends of ours, were arrested for sabotage and were jailed for between seven and fifteen years. Another ARM member, John Harris, planted a bomb in Johannesburg station on July 28, for which he telephoned a warning that, typically, was deliberately ignored by the authorities, resulting in one dead and numerous injuries. After failed pleas of clemency, he was executed on April 1, 1965, the first (and only) white to be hanged in the struggle.★

The vicelike grip of the police state on Mandela and his comrades was typified by my parents' experience. In September 1964, my father had been served with a five-year banning order similar to my mother's imposed the year before, but exceptionally allowing him to communicate with her and she with him. When still secretary of the Pretoria branch of the Liberal Party, she had been summoned in January 1963 before the chief magistrate of Pretoria and warned to desist from engaging in activities *'calculated to further the aims of communism'*. He was unable to specify which of her activities fell within this definition and advised her to write to John Vorster, minister of justice, for clarification. The reply from his private secretary merely repeated the phrase and then stated, *'Should you so wish, you are of course at liberty to ignore the warning and, if as a result thereof, it is found necessary to take further action against you, you will only have yourself to blame'*. Around this time a newspaper cartoon appeared, which had Vorster saying, *'Go and find Adelaine Hain, see what she is doing and tell her she mustn't'*.

After my father's ban had progressively prevented him from obtaining work, and as they had no private means, our family was obliged to immigrate to Britain in 1966.

⌣

On Robben Island Mandela quickly discovered that conditions had worsened since his first stay a year before. Common criminals enjoyed better conditions than "politicals" like him, who were kept in a newly completed, separate structure—a low building of rows of small cells, built around three sides of a rectangular, stone-paved courtyard, the fourth side being a high wall providing a catwalk for a warder with a gun. The Rivonia seven were all given similar cells, along one side called the Isolation Section or Section B, which looked onto the courtyard.

★Then aged fifteen, I read the address at his funeral in my school uniform after my father (subject to a banning order) had been prevented from doing so.

The six Rivonia Africans were issued with the standard short khaki trousers with no socks—"native boy" attire—but Kathrada, as an Indian, was entitled to long trousers as were Coloureds. Mandela protested about the shorts and had long trousers dumped in his cell. However, when the others were denied long trousers, he protested and had his own taken away. Only three years later were they all given long trousers.

The prisoners were woken at 5:30 a.m. to clean their cells and wash and shave in cold water from an iron bucket. They were given breakfast in the courtyard from a drum of often-stinking corn porridge together with a drink of baked corn in hot water. They worked until noon in the courtyard, sitting in rows hammering stones into gravel for long, grinding hours at a time, trying to protect their eyes from splinters, as the warders watched and shouted.

Lunch was more corn, and they then worked until 4:00 p.m., when they washed in cold seawater in a bathroom for half an hour and then had supper in their cells: more corn, sometimes with soggy vegetables or, as an occasional luxury, gristly meat. The night warder patrolled the corridor from 8:00 p.m. to ensure they were not reading or writing, but they could sometimes whisper to each other, and prisoners who were studying were soon allowed to read until later.

A bare lightbulb burned all night in every cell.

As Mandela said later, '*You have no idea of the cruelty of man against man until you have been in a South African prison with White warders and Black prisoners*'. Within weeks, he had dropped stones in weight and his skin had lost its vitality. Prisoners had no access to radio or newspapers and at first could only write and receive one letter every six months, from their immediate family.

Letters were censored—Mandela's first, from Winnie, was entirely blotted out—and censored portions were sent to the commissioner of prisons to provide political information.

Early on, their lawyers Bram Fischer and Joel Joffe were allowed to visit to try to persuade them to appeal. '*It had only been a few weeks since I had seen them, but it felt like an eternity'*, said Mandela. '*They seemed like visitors from another world'*. But neither he nor his Rivonia comrades would be shaken from their resolve not to appeal, insisting their stance of standing by what they had done was essential to the integrity of their struggle and the plight of other ANC defendants.

But he was at least with some of his closest friends and political comrades, who could reinforce each other's morale and purpose. In prison, stripped of all personal and political trappings and confined with his colleagues every day, he learned to control what had been his temper and strong will, to emphasise and persuade and to extend his influence and authority, not just over the other prisoners but also over the white warders.

In complete contrast to the common-law prisoners in other cells, the politicals were convinced of the power of their cause. Their ideas, for which they had been sent to the island, '*would never die'*. They were a remarkably disciplined, cohesive group, reinforcing each other and boosting themselves even in times of personal depression or upset. Their values and their unbending commitment to the struggle would endure and give them strength and comfort. Sisulu said they '*never lost confidence'*, despite constant privations and setbacks.

Their life quickly settled into a monotonous routine. With watches banned, they never knew the time, so Mandela established a calendar on his cell wall. Although he was to write in 1975, '*In my lifetime I shall step out into the sunshine, walk with firm feet'*, that did not mean even he would be without doubts and downs. '*I do not know that I could have done it had I been alone. But the authorities' greatest mistake was to keep us together, for together our determination was reinforced. We supported each other and gained strength from each other. . . . . Men are different and react differently to stress. But the stronger ones raised up the weaker ones, and both became stronger in the process'*.

Amid a group of powerful personalities, Mandela nevertheless stood out from the beginning. He was determined to be treated with respect and retain his self-dignity, and to achieve that, he resolved to show respect to his oppressors, to try to reach out to his jailers, however deeply he resented their harsh attitudes. He may have been a resourceful and courageous leader prepared to overthrow the state with violence, but he never wanted to dominate or humiliate his oppressors. The hand he had been dealt on the island taught him the virtues of patience and persistence. It was to become a stance that developed over the years to the point where virtually everyone who dealt with him came to admire him and treat him with some propriety, of course always subject to the necessary bounds of being an apartheid prisoner.

For his white warders—all Afrikaners with very little education who insisted on acting as masters to servants—he was a revelation. They had expected a "communist terrorist" with horns, but they found instead a proud and hugely civilized man, much better educated than they would ever be, courteous to a tee and keen to learn about them as human beings and their families, even as he was deprived of his own cherished family life.

In a way Mandela used Robben Island as a laboratory to discover how he might lead his bitterly divided country, as he continued steadfastly to believe one day he would. That meant he had to get inside the minds of his enemies, the Afrikaner, ruling *volk* (nation). In so doing he was to sweep aside conventional ANC wisdom that the Afrikaners were merely a modern version of the old white settler colonialists.

He deliberately studied Afrikaner history, coming to appreciate their enduring and intense grievance at being despised and mistreated by the British, the injustices they had suffered in the Anglo-Boer Wars and how this might explain their determination to maintain power, ironically imposing some of the very suffering on blacks that they had experienced as second-class whites. He also took a course over two years in the Afrikaner language, trying it out on his warders in their own tongue and impressing them as his proficiency gradually improved to the point where he became fluent. They were particularly taken with his knowledge of and respect for the old Boer War commanders and historic Afrikaner leaders.

In a way, what Mandela came to accept and to transmit to his captors was that his vision of a new South Africa was one in which they were "Africans" too, and that they would be a legitimate part of the future envisioned by the ANC. Although there was a deeply political and ideological strategy to all this, it was also for Mandela a way of achieving the mutual dignity and respect he wanted for himself and his comrades, over and above their subservience as prisoners under the hardest regime in the country.

Partly as a result, Mandela was treated more carefully than the others. He cut a distinctive figure on the island, displaying humility while carrying himself with a chiefly stature. When, early into their sentence, he received a visit from his lawyer, he introduced by name each of the eight astonished warders around him as his "guard of honor". But if this was all an astute accommodation to his prison environment, underneath the courtesies he displayed steel. He stood up for his fellow prisoners when they were sub-jected to pettiness, restriction or humiliation, and he was able to win concessions to improve their conditions. When one particu-larly brutal guard tried to strike him, Mandela stood erect, calmly instructing him that if he did so he would be hauled through the courts: '*And when I finish with you, you will be poor as a church mouse*'. The blow never came.

Early on, Mandela was allowed to continue his legal corre-spondence studies at London University, for which he received law books via the British Embassy, arranged by David Astor, the editor of the London *Observer*, whom he had previously met in London. He was also soon given a small table and chair in his room.

The religious services, which were conducted each Sunday by chaplains from different denominations, provided a break from the monotony of prison life, and after the third year they took place in the courtyard, which gave them the advantage of fresh air. The more long-winded the priests were, the more the prisoners liked them. Mandela listened to them all, his own faith a matter of much speculation for he was not a formal believer like Oliver Tambo and did not quote the Bible or discuss theology.

In January 1965, the prisoners' work was moved to the island's lime quarry, where they had to hack away the rock to reach the lime layers with pick and shovel. This was to be their main occupation for the next few years. There was no escape from the cold in winter or the heat in summer. Within the quarry, the sun's glare reflected off the white stone into their eyes and burned them. They were refused dark glasses for three years, and many were left with damaged eyesight; Mandela's eyes never recovered, and as he grew older he read with increasing difficulty.

As their numbers expanded, the thirty-odd political prisoners in the Isolation Section occupied a very small self-enclosed world, cut off from the rest of the prison and able to communicate only briefly with each other when they washed, at meals, and in the quarry. '*We were a universe of 30 people*', said Eddie Daniels, an ARM Liberal Party member who spent fifteen years with them. Life became like a repetitive, long-running play with, as Mandela said, '*the only audience ourselves and our oppressors*'. Daniels added, '*He gave us hope when everything was rock bottom and we saw no future. He taught me how to survive. When I was ill, he could have asked anybody else to see me. He came to me personally. He even cleaned my toilet*'.

At the core of this universe were the seven Rivonia men, who had known each other for ten to twenty years, including Mandela and his most trusted friends—Sisulu and Kathrada. Six years older than Mandela, Sisulu was still his mentor, whose clear vision, judgement, accessibility and openness to new ideas he admired. Kathrada, much the youngest of the seven and the only Indian among them, was equally steadfast, with unselfishness and inner calm. He had been a communist since his school days, but he was not dogmatic and was always loyal to Mandela, whom he called "Mdala" (the old one) out of respect. Like Sisulu, Kathrada felt free to criticize and argue with Mandela, for whom they were both mirrors through which he could see himself truthfully. The oldest and best educated was Govan Mbeki, who was, like Kathrada, a communist but, unlike him, a stubbornly Marxist one. And early in 1965, a group of guerrilla fighters arrived, including Mac Maharaj, a sophisticated Indian from Durban with a sharp mind and great courage who had suffered severe torture.

The government had decided to concentrate all nonwhite political prisoners on the island, which Mandela also thought was a great mistake because it helped rival parties to find common ground, which had never happened before. PAC prisoners were the majority of non-ANC ones, and their president Robert Sobukwe was kept in a separate house until 1969, which helped to disorient him. Many PAC prisoners bitterly resented the Indian and Coloured ANC ones, since the PAC accepted only Africans as legitimate South Africans. They also believed all the ANC to be Marxist—which of course they were not. But Mandela was determined to establish dialogue, to provide the basis for future unity outside.

Another group was from the Trotskyite Unity Movement, which had a sectarian hostility to the ANC, but its Coloured leader, Neville Alexander, soon revised his opinion of Mandela and, in the end, thought that he was *'way beyond any one of us'*.

The Coloured Liberal Eddie Daniels became one of Mandela's close friends, especially valuing the fact that Mandela took the trouble to brief Daniels personally about his meetings with visitors, so that the Liberal would not feel isolated.

Mandela's colleagues regarded him as their leader and directed visitors to his cell, as their representative. To some prisoners he still seemed governed by his past roles as traditional chief and democratic leader, but his close colleagues saw his detachment as part of his search for unity and consensus.

The ANC leaders re-created their own structure, appointing a "High Organ" of four prisoners who had served on the previous national executive as their ruling body: Mandela, Sisulu, Mbeki and their Rivonia colleague Raymond Mhlaba. The High Organ decided on policy towards prison authorities and discipline within the Isolation Section. They passed on their decisions to prisoners through a communications committee led by Kathrada, and the committee found ingenious ways to smuggle messages to political prisoners in communal cells outside the Isolation Section. These included collecting empty matchboxes, constructing false bottoms with secret messages and leaving them at points where the other political prisoners would cross their route to the lime quarry. Notes were secluded between the layers of onion skins, or wrapped in plastic at the bottom of food drums or piles of dirty dishes, left inside toilet rims and written in code on toilet paper.

He tried to be a builder, to take a position that he thinks is more suitable for a leader of the ANC.—WALTER SISULU

News was craved from outside, as the prisoners were denied newspapers and would go to extreme lengths to get one: bribing warders, stealing papers from visiting priests or retrieving the newspaper wrapping from warders' sandwiches. Mandela was once caught with a newspaper he had found on a bench and was given three days' solitary confinement on a diet of rice and water. Maharaj even managed to persuade a warder to smuggle in a newspaper, which he summarized in his tiny writing and circulated. Because Madiba was studying economics, he was allowed the *Economist* magazine for a time, but this was later withdrawn when the authorities realised it contained plenty of political analysis and news too. Mandela explained, '*The prison department tried to bury us alive by cutting us completely off from the outside world*'.

The political prisoners were worried they would disappear from the world's consciousness, and soon after their sentence this began to happen. They were almost forgotten by the media in Britain and America, and within South Africa laws forbade any mention of the ANC or its leaders, and the name of Mandela virtually disappeared. What news they did receive was depressing because, since the Rivonia trial, the police had almost wiped out any black opposition and there was scarcely an African leader who was not in jail, in exile or under a restrictive order. As Sisulu later said, '*The worst time was the 1960s*'.

When the prime minister, Hendrik Verwoerd, was assassinated in Parliament by a messenger in September 1966, the political prisoners heard the shocking news in a whisper from one of the ordinary prisoners in the quarry. Verwoerd's successor, John Vorster, a man who had been imprisoned during the war for pro-Nazi treason, brought in the 1967 Terrorism Act, giving the police even more draconian powers, and in 1969 he established a new secret service organization—the Bureau of State Security (BOSS)—which quickly embarked on renewed tactics of state terror.

Mandela felt powerless to influence affairs on the mainland and followed what little news he could get with increasing frustration.

The prisoners had agreed not to try to interfere with the decisions of the ANC in exile, but Mandela did have fitful contact with Oliver Tambo via smuggled coded messages, maintaining his trust in Tambo, which became a key to the ANC's unity and eventual success.

Mandela's main concern was the progress of the ANC's armed struggle, and in October 1967, when the prisoners learned from the *Economist* that their soldiers were fighting along the Zambia-Rhodesia border, their hopes rose. The MK detachment, assisted by Zimbabwean guerrillas, fought the white Rhodesian army, but they were eventually overcome when South African army units arrived. He and his comrades were thrilled when captured guerrillas later arrived on the island and regaled them with exciting stories of the fighting.

However, in 1969, after internal criticisms of Tambo for failures in the guerrilla campaign, the ANC meeting in exile agreed for the first time to admit non-Africans, including the white communist Joe Slovo who became MK's commander. This encouraged the Robben Islanders but caused problems for Tambo by reviving suspicions that white communists were running the organization.

Meanwhile, Tambo's hopes of assistance from black Africa were fading. The economic and military strength of South Africa helped it to bully or seduce the much poorer black nations to the north, which depended on it for trade, access to the sea and migrant jobs. The United Nations, with new African members, and the Organization for African Unity founded in 1963 promised boycotts and aid, and Zambia and Tanzania became the champions of black liberation. But when fourteen heads of African states met in Zambia in May 1969, their "Lusaka Manifesto", drafted without consulting the ANC, disappointingly stressed the need for compromise with South Africa and played down the armed struggle.

By the mid-1960s, the withdrawal of foreign capital after Sharpeville had been reversed, and Tambo's overseas campaign against apartheid became harder. South Africa's growth rate averaged 6 percent higher than all Western nations, increasing demand for black workers and encouraging the prevalent view in the West that prosperity would inevitably compel reforms and that whites would become more liberal—a stance vigorously opposed by the growing anti-apartheid movements and flying in the face of all the evidence.

The ANC was training more guerrillas in camps outside South Africa and sending in propaganda through leaflets or broadcasts over *Radio Freedom* from Zambia and Tanzania. To Tambo, an eventual bloodbath now seemed almost inevitable, and from Robben Island the outlook also seemed grimmer. In the all-white 1970 general election, there was no sign of the promised liberalization; indeed, the less reactionary, English-dominated United Party was routed. Resistance inside South Africa seemed to have disappeared, and Western governments and observers had written off the ANC. When the *Washington Post* correspondent was in South Africa in 1970, he found that the Robben Island leaders were perceived dimly, '*as if they belonged to another time, long passed and long lost*'.

—

A great problem for the political prisoners was how they should relate to the warders, who dominated their daily lives and had the power to prosecute them. These were usually young rural Afrikaners, many from poor or broken homes, much less well educated and confident than the politicals and therefore more insecure, resentful and obsessed with the rules, living in their own kind of prison on the bleak island.

Mandela was aware from his earlier periods in jail that he could impress warders with a combination of assertiveness, respect and legal knowledge, and that he could retain his dignity in the most humiliating circumstances. He would respect them as human beings but would never be subservient. He would ensure that prisoners set their own pace of work and would never call the guards "baas" (boss), as they demanded.

He recognized that when the prisoners had a good relationship with warders who dealt with them, '*it became difficult for the higher-ups to treat you roughly*', and he soon realised that the warders '*were not homogeneous; that there was a debate between those who treated the prisoners humanely and those determined to see that the prisoners would never again resist White supremacy*'. He was always hopeful of converting them and said, '*I soon realized that when an Afrikaner changes he changes completely and becomes a real friend*'. Sisulu saw these talks as the precursor to the eventual discussions with the government, of which he later said, '*The negotiation itself was a process that started from this source*'.

Of the few foreign visitors who were allowed to visit the political prisoners, most seem to have been unsympathetic to the ANC, and one British journalist actually wrote on his return that conditions on Robben Island were better than in many prisons he had visited in Britain! However, after hearing stories of the wretched conditions, Helen Suzman, the Progressive Party parliamentarian, insisted on visiting. She was taken to Mandela's cell, where he told her about the poor food and clothing, about the lack of newspapers and books and about a brutal warder with a swastika tattoo, while the prison commander and the commissioner of prisons listened. '*Mandela had a commanding presence over both prisoners and warders, no doubt about it'*, Suzman said, and soon after her visit improvements started.

By 1967, the prisoners' treatment was relatively civilized and relaxed: they could wear long trousers and sweaters in winter, they could talk in the quarry and the courtyard, and sometimes they received eggs and fruit. But the diet was still minimal, and there were no newspapers.

Suzman was to visit Mandela in prison seven more times, each time having lively political arguments. Her party did not support one-person one-vote, and they could never agree about the use of violence. In 1969, on her second visit, she asked Mandela to say that he would abandon violence, and when he would not, she refused to ask for his release. But the prisoners were always grateful for her practical help.

By 1970, Mandela had obviously become the spokesman for the political prisoners from all parties, and in January he wrote a long letter of complaint to the commissioner on behalf of all the prisoners, which ended urging him *'to act with speed and take appropriate measures to relieve the situation before matters go out of control'*.

Instead, the government responded at the end of that year by appointing a new prison commanding officer, Colonel Piet Badenhorst, who arrived with a reputation for brutality—and some thuggish new warders. The guards now seized any excuse to persecute the prisoners, depriving them of meals and refusing reading of anything not relevant to their studies. Badenhorst soon stopped them from studying anything because, he said, they were lazy, and he refused to talk to Mandela. Kathrada wrote, *'They have launched a sort of reign of terror'*. At the end of May 1971, "the terror" reached a climax on the evening of the tenth anniversary of the republic.

On May 28, a group of drunken warders, including the sadistic head warder Carstens, burst into the cells, told everyone to strip naked and kept them with their hands up for half an hour while they searched every cell. Mbeki collapsed and was taken to hospital in Cape Town. They could hear the warders beating up prisoners in adjoining cells, hitting them and twisting their testicles; one was battered to the floor and then made to clean up his blood-spattered cell.

The prisoners never learned the reason for this but suspected the warders had been provoked by some bad political news—Maharaj said that their brutality was always linked to some external event that threatened the warders' view of their country—'*whether guerrillas, rugby or border troubles*'. The warders were especially incensed at news of the stopping in May 1970 of the white South African cricket tour to Britain, following militant protests that had earlier severely disrupted a rugby tour by their beloved Springboks. This confirms the effect sports protests and boycotts had upon white South Africans, especially Afrikaners, and of which, when leading such campaigns in Britain, I had been all too well aware. When he eventually came out from prison, Mandela told me how hugely important our campaigns had been.

The brutality hammered down on the politicals for a year, with warders confiscating their precious books (in Mandela's case including Shakespeare and Greek classics) and instituting beatings whenever they wanted. But throughout all this prison terror Mandela remained calm, and Daniels was convinced his authoritative presence saved him and others from many assaults. Frustrated and angry though they all were, Mandela urged his comrades to bide their time.

The moment came after he led a delegation to see Badenhorst, threatening strikes if their conditions were not improved. A month later, three judges arrived with the commissioner of prisons. The judges asked to see Mandela privately, but he insisted that Badenhorst should be present. When Mandela described the brutal beating of a prisoner, Badenhorst burst out, '*If you talk of things you haven't seen, you will get yourself into trouble*'. Mandela, the lawyer in him, quickly pounced as if addressing a court: '*If he can threaten me here in your presence, you can imagine what he does when you are not here*'. The judges had to acknowledge his logic.

After this, conditions improved, and within three months Badenhorst, the tormentor of the politicals, was told he would be transferred together with his brutal gang of warders. But just before he departed, and in another twist that made a profound impact upon Mandela, Badenhorst said privately to him, '*I just want to wish you people good luck*'. Dumbfounded, Mandela quickly reciprocated by wishing him all the best in his new post. The Afrikaner oppressor and the African victim had somehow found a common bond, and Mandela was to build upon this insight in the future.

Some of the prisoners saw the warders as slaves of the system, but Mandela went further—he could see beyond the brutalities to the insecurities and psychological deformities of the warders—and he was already seeing the prison as a microcosm of a future South Africa, where reconciliation would be essential to survival and progress.

By the 1970s, conditions on Robben Island, though still grim, were not hellish. The balance of power had begun changing in December 1971, when a new head of prison was appointed to replace the hated Badenhorst. Colonel Willie Willemse, with a gentlemanly style, had been told by the prisons commissioner to adopt a more enlightened approach, because the government had to reckon with the political scene at home and abroad, where there was now a rising profile for Mandela and his comrades amid a growing international anti-apartheid movement.

Some twenty-five years later, Willemse said, '*I made myself accessible. . . . I recognized they were political leaders*'. Most of the prisoners respected him, and he knew that he couldn't control any of them without their cooperation, particularly Mandela. Already, as Mandela said, '*the inmates, not the authorities, seemed to be running the prison*'. There were now fewer warders to supervise them, and they had virtually stopped working. As Kathrada commented in 1971, '*We just go to the quarry and do nothing*'. When Willemse appealed to Mandela to help impose some discipline in the quarry, Mandela persuaded the prisoners to resume work—but at their own pace.

The Red Cross was now playing a discreet role in improving prison conditions, and just before it visited in 1972 the prisoners were issued with two new sets of underwear; by 1973, there was hot water for washing and showers. Mandela was now allowed three letters and two visits a month, and also a special bed and a salt-free diet for his high blood pressure. After more requests, prisoners were allowed spells of alternative work away from the quarry, and they were taken to the seashore to collect seaweed. For the first time in years, they saw the ocean and, with Table Mountain across the bay, the city of Cape Town, where life went on.

By then, the prisoners had been given the opportunity to study, and this was most precious to them. Mandela had urged the commissioner to '*let the atmosphere of a university prevail*', and soon this was happening and the quarry became a kind of campus for what was to be called the "University of Robben Island".

Anyone with a degree or qualification would teach his subject—Mandela taught political economy—and each morning they would plan their courses at the quarry. They could present their lessons, or lectures, swinging a pick or digging lime. But as the work became more relaxed or stopped altogether, they would stand in groups with different classes in progress. Some prisoners were illiterate when they came to the island. Govan Mbeki explained, '*We took people from the lowest level . . . and they had to be taught, and by the time they left Robben Island they were able to write letters home . . . and they spoke English*'. Many progressed to more formal studies through correspondence schools. Some took university degrees. The prisoners' isolation provided a unique opportunity for continuous and organized study, protected from all the interruptions and distractions of normal urban life. Some young warders were also infected by the educational atmosphere, and Willemse later said that the island '*was a university for the warders too*'.

The warders became less strict in supervising the prisoners, allowing them to talk as they worked, and the quarry became not only a campus but also a debating club, especially for political opinions. There were real differences within the High Organ.

Mandela and Sisulu were often at odds with Mbeki, the convinced Marxist, which sometimes led to strained relations. The conciliators were also criticized by other Marxists on the island who, by 1975, were starting to challenge Mandela's leadership and resurrecting the old arguments from the pre-jail period. After 1975, the question of Mandela's leadership was put to all members of the ANC and the sister congresses outside, who reaffirmed it with an overwhelming vote of support.

In December 1974, Mandela had a surprise visit from the notorious minister of justice, Jimmy Kruger, who tried unsuccessfully to persuade him to abandon the armed struggle. Mandela found Kruger to be crude, ignorant and unsophisticated—he knew nothing of the ANC and had never heard of the Freedom Charter. Kruger wanted Mandela to recognize the legitimacy of the Transkei "Bantustan" government under Mandela's old friend Kaiser Matanzima with whom he had fallen out twenty years before. Mandela wouldn't and gave the same answers when Kruger returned a month later. Shortly afterward, the minister attacked Mandela in Parliament as a card-carrying communist.

Meanwhile, Sisulu and Kathrada thought that Mandela should write his autobiography as a means of focusing attention on their struggle, and in 1975 Maharaj suggested it should be published on his sixtieth birthday in 1978. It was a mammoth undertaking. He would have a sleep during the day and then write energetically during the night, turning out a long book with many details in four months. Some sections were letters to his daughter Zeni, and he told her he was working to a strict deadline: '*Every completed sheet must leave the prison daily and I never see it again*'. So Maharaj received ten pages of foolscap from him every day. Mandela could not refer to any previous pages so had to keep in his mind what he had already written, together with his train of thought—an extraordinary feat, as any author will know.

Maharaj copied Mandela's sheets in writing less than half a millimeter high and concealed the small pages among his study books, giving Mandela's originals to Sisulu and Kathrada for comments and corrections. He then hid the revised miniature sheets inside a book of statistics, which he planned to smuggle out when he finished his sentence in 1976. The originals were kept as a standby in three plastic containers buried under the courtyard. There they remained hidden until other prisoners began digging there for the foundations of a new wall. Mandela and friends managed to destroy two of the containers, but the third was found and sent to the commanding officer.

After a long delay, the commissioner of prisons wrote a confidential report to his minister in October 1977, explaining that this "undesirable literature" had been found and verified by handwriting experts as having been written by Mandela, with additions by Maharaj and Kathrada. He summarized the ten chapters and, since the paper used had been supplied to the prisoners for studying, suggested that their study privileges be permanently withdrawn. In the end, Mandela, Sisulu and Kathrada were stopped from studying for four years. In 1976, the miniature pages were taken out by Maharaj and sent to London, where they were typed and forwarded to Oliver Tambo. The autobiography remained unpublished and disappeared for almost twenty years until, in 1994, it provided the basis for the first two-thirds of Mandela's inspirational autobiography, *Long Walk to Freedom*.

—

In April 1974, the Robben Islanders received a boost to their morale: a military coup in Portugal, which ousted its fascist regime, followed by the independence of the two nearby Portuguese colonies, Angola and Mozambique. The ANC saw the possibility of military bases in Mozambique, along the South African border, supported by the country's new revolutionary black government, FRELIMO, and Mandela felt confident that at last '*the tide was turning our way*'.

But Vorster was flexible enough to work with the new black government in Mozambique, continuing to use that country's ports and provide jobs for migrant workers in return for the absence of military activity. By now the economic boom had subsided and South Africa's businessmen urgently needed markets in the rest of Africa. Vorster paid a secret visit to the Ivory Coast and Liberia, and brought pressure on Ian Smith to negotiate with the black rebel movements in Rhodesia. At the UN in November 1974, the South African foreign minister Pik Botha said his country was set on reform: *'We shall do everything in our power to move away from discrimination based on race or color'*. But Mandela was convinced there would be no fundamental changes.

Abroad, Tambo was in a difficult position. When Albert Luthuli died in 1967, the ANC national executive elected Tambo as president in Mandela's absence, but he still called himself "acting president" and referred to Mandela as "commander in chief" and president-in-waiting to whom he would defer. For his part Mandela was preoccupied with maintaining unity, both within the ANC and with its partners. There were growing tensions in the ANC in exile, again between nationalists and communists. Tambo was now under fire and worried about further splits. Mandela had to smuggle out a message urging solidarity with Tambo as the ANC's de facto leader.

The ANC also faced difficult obstacles in the West. Anti-apartheid genuflections by the US and British governments belied the reality of complicity with the white regime through continued trade and support on the side. Although Senator Robert Kennedy paid a visit to South Africa in 1966, and said, *'If I lived in this country . . . I would get out now'*, his was a lone radical voice and the election of Richard Nixon's Republican administration saw the easing of an arms embargo from 1969. The return of a Conservative British government in 1970 also saw the resumption of arms sales cut off by their Labour predecessors and renewed support for the British naval base at Simonstown on the Cape Peninsula. When eight days of US Senate committee hearings about South Africa were held in 1976, the name of Mandela was never uttered—only the black congressman from Atlanta, Andrew Young, argued, *'If there is a rational solution to the problem of South Africa, it is going to have to be worked out with those men who are now imprisoned or detained or now being destroyed'*.

The Robben Islanders put more hope in the East. The Soviet Union and Eastern Europe continued to welcome ANC leaders, to provide funds and weaponry for their armed struggle and to educate ANC exiles at their universities. Tambo was impressed that Moscow did not try to pressure ANC policy, and he kept his distance from any communist influence. Sisulu and others believed their salvation would come from the socialist world; Mandela believed the ANC should work with any friends it could find. His ideas about basic strategy were becoming stronger: he saw the armed struggle as central to liberation but felt sanctions would play '*a very important subsidiary role*' by depriving the regime of support from international trade and investment. He was also hopeful that the by-now near universal international sports boycott could act as a catalyst for change among sports-mad whites.

Social change within South Africa was slowly weakening apartheid and widening the opposition to it. The sources of unrest were the factories, where the bad economic situation in the early 1970s had caused black workers to demand higher wages, triggering strikes despite the fact that they were illegal. The workers' broad movement had no formal leaders to be picked up and victimized. Semiskilled black employees could not easily be replaced, and they quickly won wage increases, which made them interested in trade unions. Welcoming this, Mandela said early in 1976 that their defiant attitude showed that in the factories '*they were no longer prepared to tolerate any kind of discrimination*'.

He was also encouraged by the opposition to apartheid from white liberals, churchmen and students, and hoped that the new Progressive Party, which had six MPs elected in the 1974 elections, would help to educate whites about the evils of discrimination. He was determined to open up lines to Afrikaners, more so after his contacts with warders. In a paper warning his colleagues not to reject any dealings with Afrikaners, he was already anticipating the opportunity that would arise fifteen years later: '*Honest men are to be found on both sides of the color line, and the Afrikaner is no exception*'.

Another critical development Mandela had first heard from

Winnie. Talking in her coded language during a visit, she described a new generation of militant black rebels who were emerging inside South Africa, and she warned him to take them seriously—she was attracted to both their ideas and their young leaders. The "Black Consciousness" movement had begun in 1969, when a young medical student, Steve Biko, turned against the white leadership of the National Union of South African Students and formed the all-black South African Students Organization (SASO), which soon led to a new party—the Black People's Convention (BPC). Biko felt blacks were diminished by the paternalism of white liberals and must escape from their sense of inferiority so that they became '*self-defined, not as defined by others*'. Some of the rhetoric sounded similar to the Youth League revolt twenty-five years before, or the PAC ten years before. But Biko had gained more confidence and intellectual depth from the independence of black Africa, the civil rights victories in America, and the growing literature of "black power".

He soon excited a militant generation of black schoolchildren who saw their parents in this humiliating image and were determined to escape from it. Black Consciousness was sweeping through the black campuses by 1973, and the government banned eight of its leaders, including Biko.

Mandela and colleagues were doubtful when they first heard about Black Consciousness, partly because Afrikaners welcomed this as a sign that blacks were '*developing on their own lines*'.

Despite this, Winnie Mandela (then banned from active politics) was inspired by the anger and assertiveness of the young rebels. Biko, from the Eastern Cape, always tried to see Winnie when he was in Johannesburg, and she said of him, '*It was such a revitalizing experience to communicate with that man . . . . I was the only voice at that time that was brave enough to do so*'. She shared the new pride in blackness: '*You felt proud of being Black, and that is what Steve did to me*'. When her bans expired in 1975, Winnie gave speeches and interviews warning about a surge of anger among young blacks.

All in all, the Black man has become a shell, a shadow of man, completely defeated, drowning in his own misery, a slave and ox bearing the yoke of oppression with sheepish timidity.
—STEVE BIKO

⁓

If Mandela had been gradually winning his political struggle inside prison, he was constantly pained by his disconnection from his family outside, especially his inability to exercise his duties as husband and father. This left him bereft and also meant Winnie, though by now a political figure in her own right, felt terribly isolated and vulnerable, the butt of white hostility and police intolerance as the symbol still at large in the country of the iconic ogre on the island. All the while, she was trying to survive and bring up their two girls.

She was, decades later, sadly to become engulfed in swirling allegations of criminality, her personal life highly controversial, and then to be tragically divorced from the man whom she had loved and sacrificed so much for, and who in turn had cherished and pined after her every day on the island. But in the beginning, and for long years to come, there was never a hint of all this. How she coped with the grinding, sometimes incurably petty, ubiquitously oppressive apartheid system determined to crush her indomitable spirit rightly invoked huge admiration, as did her striking stance as a modern, independently minded woman in a highly traditional, male-dominated culture (both white and black).

Mandela as a political prisoner was allowed just one visitor every six months, and Winnie's first came three months into his sentence in 1964. Like all such visits by the wives of the politicals, it was plagued by officialdom and problems. As a banned person, she needed special permission to travel outside her home area of Orlando as well as special permission from the minister of justice himself to talk to her banned husband, which she was otherwise prevented from doing.

Sometimes the wives might have only a day's notice that a visit was possible. Or they might have planned a visit in advance on information given, only to find the necessary permit would be delayed until after the scheduled plane had departed. Because of all this, coupled with the long distances and costs of travel, some of the politicals received no visit from a loved one for more than ten years. In 1966, Winnie was charged with violating prison regulations for a visit after going by plane, instead of by specified train, which she had to do to get there before her visit permit expired.

She came that first time with Sisulu's wife Albertina, covering nearly a thousand miles (1,600 km) to reach Cape Town Docks, where they signed the prison visitors book, agreeing to all manner of restrictions. Alighting from the ferry they were marched to a waiting room, with little sight of the prison environment their men inhabited. Contact visits for politicals were prohibited, so Winnie was shown into a cramped room, with Mandela in the next room, connected by a small, thick and opaque window with a warder-controlled telephone for conversation. There he saw her, lovely and vivaciously dressed as she always would be for him on such occasions. Two warders stood behind her and three behind him. Anything that might stray onto the political would be quickly interrupted. Mandela said, '*It was tremendously frustrating not to be able to touch my wife, to speak tenderly to her, to have a private moment together*', as they talked about the girls, their schooling and the family circumstances.

Winnie was obviously under enormous strain. Mandela was shocked to discover that she had received a second banning order and had been sacked from the child welfare officer job she loved. He was deeply troubled by the way she was being harassed: '*I could not look after her and the children, and the state was making it difficult for her to look after herself. My powerlessness gnawed at me*'. Suddenly, it was time up—the thirty permitted minutes had come abruptly to an end, and she was hustled out, the last time they would see each other for two full years.

She went home to tell their daughters about seeing the father they did not know and could not remember. Not only had they been separated from their father, but also they were now increasingly kept away from their mother too, as tougher banning orders imposed still more restrictions, including visiting schools or any African area outside Orlando. As Winnie described, '*I was never there as a mother to hold my little girls' hands, take them to school and introduce them to their teachers, as is the glory of every mother when her children are starting school*'. Partly because even meeting the girls' teachers would have meant violating her ban, she was forced to place them at an early age in a boarding school.

Police intimidation on her employers also continue to dog her attempts to work, as she tried various menial jobs in retail and cleaning, now that she could no longer be a social worker. From a shy country girl she had become a buoyant and beautiful woman as well as an increasingly prominent political activist—but one subject to intolerable pressures of loneliness and state harassment, made worse by what friends described as her tendency to be overtrusting as she discovered that two imagined friends turned out to be police informers.

The security police even spread a lie that she herself was an informer, making very sure that Mandela was fed the gossip through the otherwise blanket ban on information getting to the island.

Winnie was painfully ostracized by their political colleagues, which Mandela had to somehow combat by smuggling out a message demanding that his wife be supported as she continued to be intimidated. Police raided their home in May 1969, arresting her under the 1967 Terrorism Act, which provided for indefinite detention without charge. She was placed in solitary confinement, beaten, aggressively interrogated and six months later, charged with twenty-two others under the Suppression of Communism Act for trying to reorganize the ANC. Finally, in September 1970, fully seventeen months after her imprisonment, she was acquitted and released.

Mandela, though able to get a message out ensuring Winnie was properly represented by top lawyers, had sleepless nights: '*There was nothing I found so agonizing in prison as the thought that Winnie was in prison too. Although I often urged others not to worry about what they could not control, I was unable to take my own advice. What were the authorities doing to my wife? How would she bear up? Who was looking after our daughters? Who would pay the bills?*'

Soon after her acquittal, Winnie's banning order was renewed for five years, with fresh restrictions placing her under "house arrest" each night and during weekends, and visitors were forbidden. This made even normal life—let alone any political life—impossible, as would become quickly evident when she was accused of violating her banning order by receiving visitors, in this case relatives including children who called unexpectedly at her house, or when her daughters were brought from boarding school by a friend to see her, the encounter also breaking the regulations. Over the next few years, she was in and out of court and prison, the ubiquitous special branch constantly on her tail, ready to pounce on the most minor breach of the straitjacket imposed upon her.

For Mandela, even as conditions on the island eased, the plight of his wife and family made these years deeply troubling. In spring 1968, he had been visited by his mother for the first time in more than four years, and she appeared haggard and ill. It was not long before he received a telegram that she had died of a heart attack, but he was denied permission to attend her funeral. A year later, in July 1969, he got further heartbreaking news that his oldest son by his first marriage, Thembi, then a father of two, had been killed in a car crash. '*I returned to my cell and lay on my bed. I do not know how long I stayed there. Finally Walter came to me and knelt beside my bed, and I gave him the telegram. He said nothing, but only held my hand. I do not know how long he remained with me. There is nothing one can say to another at such a time'*. He was again denied permission to attend the funeral.

For Winnie, the intolerable continued, as the authorities became increasingly upset at her growing popularity, especially among young blacks; her courageous and proud defiance of the restrictive tentacles she faced inspired many of her compatriots. In 1974, she was arrested and detained for breaking her banning orders and sentenced to six months' imprisonment. But to Mandela's relief, after her release she was able to visit Robben Island, for the first time with their youngest daughter Zindzi, now in her mid-teens. He had not seen her since she was tiny and was thrilled at *'what a beautiful woman my youngest daughter had become'*. There was an understandable awkwardness about the encounter, which Mandela tried to break by telling her stories of how he used to play with her as a baby and how she seldom cried: *'Through the glass'*, he recalled, *'I could see her holding back her tears as I talked'*.

But all these terrible strains on the family were as nothing compared with when, in the early hours of May 16, 1977, Winnie was forcibly taken and interrogated in a police station, where she gave as good as she got. No longer the shrinking violet of her youth, she returned the police insults with those of her own. Then she was told abruptly that she was being banished to the Orange Free State, an Afrikaner heartland, where life for blacks was nasty, brutish, and all too often short. Zindzi was brought to join her as she was taken from the prison back home; its contents were literally uprooted—precious possessions, crockery, Mandela's books and furniture alike—and thrown in the back of an army truck.

She and Zindzi were herded with heavily armed soldiers into the back of another truck and in convoy driven some 250 miles (400 km) to the southwest of Johannesburg and dumped in a desolate township outside the small, parochial white town Brandfort. Her new house made their small box in Orlando seem positively palatial. There were piles of soil on the floor, which had to be cleared out, no running water, no cooker, three small rooms and doors so tiny that none of her furniture could be got in and had to be stored in the local police station. With no food or water, she curled up in misery with Zindzi on a mattress on bare earth, and they tried to sleep. She said afterward, '*It was terrible. For Zindzi, it was traumatic. Worse things have happened to people in the struggle, but it was the hardest thing for me to take as a mother, that your commitment affects those who are very dear to you. That shattering experience inflicted a wound that will never heal. Of course I was bitter, more than I have ever been*'.

As for her husband, far away in prison, she said of both her and her daughters, '*We never had him physically to share that love he exudes so much of. I knew when I married him that I married the struggle, the liberation of my people*'.

Among Mandela's regular letters to her were two poignant ones about growing a tomato plant. Almost from the outset on Robben Island, Mandela had tried to get permission for a small garden, for he saw growing plants from seeds as offering '*a small taste of freedom*'. For years the authorities resisted this but eventually conceded, to Mandela's delight, for he saw gardening somewhat metaphorically.

He wrote to Winnie how he had carefully husbanded an especially lovely tomato plant so that it produced good fruit. But then it started to wither and die, and however much he tried there was nothing he could do to bring it back to life. He was never sure what she read into his lengthy and detailed tale of the tomato plant, but he wrote it with mixed feelings: '*I did not want our relationship to go the way of that plant, and yet I felt that I had been unable to nourish many of the most important relationships in my life. Sometimes there is nothing one can do to save something that must die*'.

· 6 ·

Resistance

$\mathscr{A}$s the intolerable treatment of Winnie Mandela confirmed, the apartheid superstructure and its feared security apparatus remained firmly in place. With Nelson Mandela and his Rivonia comrades entering their second decade on the island, white South Africa had been enjoying a better international press than usual in the two years to mid-1976, as so-called petty apartheid was ameliorated. Whites-only signs were reported being removed from some park benches; black athletes were pictured competing against whites on select occasions to try to break through the strong solid sports boycott; and John Vorster, the prime minister, was courted as peacemaker in the Rhodesian deadlock. Apartheid's propaganda machine had reason to be pleased with itself.

Suddenly that illusion was shattered by a six-letter word: Soweto. Now a complex of twenty-eight townships including Orlando, where the Mandelas had their small home, Soweto had no electricity, no proper shops and no modern amenities—just vast numbers of boxlike concrete houses with water and drainage; the official population of six hundred thousand had risen to be well over a million.

On the morning of June 16, 1976, white policemen fired on schoolchildren protesting peacefully against an edict the previous year forcing them to be taught in Afrikaans. They had been carrying placards with slogans such as "Down with Afrikaans", "Blacks

Are Not Dustbins", "Afrikaans Stinks", "Afrikaans Is Tribal Language" and "Bantu Education—To Hell with It."

The first child to be killed was thirteen-year-old Hector Pietersen, whose photograph was flashed around the world as he died being carried by his crying brother. The township exploded—police vehicles were stoned and set on fire, police dogs unleashed upon students were knifed, official buildings and vehicles were burned and looted and two white officials were killed. A storm of resistance was unleashed, with Soweto in the middle and virtually under martial law as an occupied territory. On four days in August, the students organized work boycotts—stay-at-homes—by Soweto workers, which seriously crippled business in Johannesburg. Shock waves tore through the country as black communities took to the streets in a display of defiance at the hated white oppression greater even than that which followed the Sharpeville massacre sixteen years before. It met with a predictable response: protesters shot down mercilessly, in the back, the head and the chest. By the end of the year, more than six hundred were dead and over six thousand had been arrested.

Although the hated Afrikaans decree was withdrawn, many pupils fled to escape the police. Apartheid-sponsored administrative bodies in Soweto collapsed amid the agitation organized by the now-powerful Soweto Students Representative Council, and a new movement of Black Consciousness organizations developed, with a new generation of activists and militants. Then, on September 12, 1977, there was further outrage when their leader, Steve Biko, died in police custody in Pretoria. He had suffered brain damage from a police beating in a cell in Port Elizabeth and was then transported naked on the floor of a police van for some six hundred miles (960 km).

Biko, by now a symbol of internal black resistance, was the forty-sixth political prisoner to die in police custody, and especially since the police tried to cover it up, his death provoked international outrage. Anti-apartheid movements stepped up campaigns, giving expression to universal outrage, and many more activists slipped into exile to join the ANC and MK, now well enough established in the frontline states to be able to give them thorough guerrilla training.

The government had blamed the unrest on the ANC, the PAC and communists, but the inspiration came from Biko and the schoolboy leaders themselves, who knew little of the ANC. Winnie had been in Soweto when Pietersen was killed and said later, '*I was part of that revolution. . . . It was the contribution of those children who put us where we are today*'. When, immediately after the first riots, a Black Parents Association was formed in Soweto to liaise with the children, Winnie was the only woman on the executive. Their family doctor, Nthatho Motlana, also on the executive, was astonished at her fearlessness and physical strength, and he commented that '*she is not scared of anything!*'

Accounts gradually filtered through to the island, and Mandela wrote a statement that Mac Maharaj smuggled out when he was released soon afterward. It showed Mandela's militant support for the revolt, and concluded, '*Unite! Mobilize! Fight on! Between the anvil of united mass action and the hammer of armed struggle we shall crush apartheid and White minority racist rule!*'

The first detailed news reached the prisoners in August 1976, when young Black Consciousness rebels, defiant and aggressive, started to flood onto the island, many having been savagely tortured. Others from MK training camps had returned as fighters and been captured. A key figure, "Terror" Lekota (nicknamed for his fearsome reputation on the football field), found the political prisoners '*steadfast in their fight*' but out of touch, and he thought '*the Rivonia people were old conservatives, and that the PAC was more appealing with its call of Africa for the Africans*'.

However, Mandela was impressed by the young rebels and realised the ANC was being challenged to catch up. The extent of the generation gap was a shock to him and his comrades, as they suddenly found themselves looking very old and moderate, and he was shaken to find that these rebels were almost as cynical about the ANC as they were of the government, some having been told

Soweto, June 1976. School children protesting.

that Mandela was a "sellout". For Mandela this *'was a novel and not altogether pleasant feeling'*, so he asked some of the young rebels to give lectures to the older prisoners, trying all the time to relate to the impatient, angry young men whom he needed to bring into the broader movement. Many of them he found sectarian and immature in their preoccupation with blackness and exclusion of whites, but he was careful not to respond aggressively, nor to campaign for the ANC or try to recruit from the new organizations. Instead, he and his comrades set about trying to convert the young comrades to more strategic and moderate policies.

Most of the rebels came to admire the resilience of the veterans, surprised that after so many years on the island they *'were still so courageous, mentally alert and determined to fight on'*, as one put it. Some of them still regarded Mandela as a sellout because he had reached understandings with the warders. But they gradually came to recognize many of the warders as human and vulnerable, especially to jokes, as the veterans' influence gradually took effect.

'After four to six months, the excitement died down', recalled Lekota, who was himself a critical influence. Before coming to the island he knew little about the ANC, although he had read Mandela's speech at the Rivonia trial; since then, he had only ever heard Mandela's name spoken in whispers. When Lekota arrived, he smuggled Mandela a note asking some political questions, and Mandela wrote back with three pages of the ANC's history. *'I read it over and over'*, Lekota remembered, *'and I knew I'd join the ANC'*.

Mandela was impressed by this strong, articulate young leader and advised him not to leave his own South African Student Organization. But Lekota was determined to do so, his switch provoking one of his Black Consciousness comrades to set upon him with a garden fork, hitting him on the head and nearly killing him. The prison authorities charged the culprit with assault, but Mandela and Walter Sisulu wanted to avoid an open rift and asked Lekota not to make a complaint. He refused to testify, which undermined the charge and brought him closer both to Mandela and to the younger activists. Many other young comrades soon followed Lekota into the ANC—including his attacker.

A crucial catalyst in the unifying process was sport, which had first been allowed in 1967 and had developed into an elaborate system of teams and tournaments, under the supervision of the Robben Island Amateur Athletic Association. Football matches were very popular, and sport helped to impose discipline; the organization of sports extended into choirs, musical groups, films and ballroom dancing. A prisoner who came to the island as '*a rural village boy*' said, '*The way we lived on Robben Island, you became an all-rounder*'. Mandela saw sport primarily as a way to overcome political rivalries. The teams were originally divided into ANC, PAC and so on, but they were later integrated, so sport and culture could avoid political deadlocks—members of different organizations could be seen sitting together talking earnestly and cracking jokes about everything except politics.

But there were still clashes between Black Consciousness (BC) and PAC prisoners, and the ANC. Mandela continued to worry about the divisiveness of BC prisoners who continued to attack the ANC's multiracialism. Two years after Soweto, he wrote a lucid, fifty-five-page essay, never published, that analyzed the roots and significance of the BC movement. He decided that the BC students were heavily influenced by the international student revolt of the 1960s, together with the American campaigns against the Vietnam War. He felt their ideas had been imported from America and '*swallowed in a lump*' without any understanding of the different conditions in South Africa, where whites had joined the liberation movement. By adopting the American concept of black power, the BC movement '*assumed the character of a racialist sect which blindly bundles a section of the progressive forces with the enemy*'.

Mandela was also impatient with the arrogance of some BC prisoners and was worried that they might in future become collaborators, supported by Western imperialists to counter communism and liberalism in black politics. He reasserted his belief in "scientific socialism" and insisted that '*the socialist countries are the best friends of those who fought for national liberation*'. The ANC had been dominated throughout its history by noncommunists, and Mandela said,

We can tame the most ultra-leftist radical just as we can rebuff the rightist elements who glibly warn us of communist danger and who at the same time collaborate with our enemies.

⁓

The response from whites to the Soweto uprising had been characteristically intransigent. In the general election in late September 1976, the Nationalists were returned with an increased majority, and Prime Minister Vorster made it plain that the fundamentals of apartheid would continue. But regardless of his public stance, Vorster knew that a policy of no change was unsustainable. After Soweto, capital left the country, businesses collapsed and the housing market went into sharp decline. Whites were in a despondent state and could see no way ahead.

For the first two decades of apartheid, there had been sufficient white workers to fill most skilled jobs and hundreds of thousands of blacks had been removed from towns. But then the growth in manufacturing overtook the capacity of the white population to produce skilled workers, especially as the government's vigorous "Afrikaner-first" policies had moved many Afrikaners out of blue-collar jobs and into the traditionally English-dominated civil service, which was, by the end of the 1970, almost 90 percent Afrikaans.

As a consequence, factory managers could not find the white workers that the apartheid laws said they must employ, so they evaded the law by promoting whites who had previously done the job and calling them "supervisors", and then recruiting black workers at lower wages to do the work. Job titles were altered to conceal the fact that blacks were doing whites' work. Furthermore, the official line demanding the reduction in the flow of blacks to towns—instead to be returned to, or to remain settled in, their so-called homelands—contradicted the needs of industry, which was drawing blacks in their thousands into towns. The newcomers settled in shanty towns or caused overcrowding in township houses—illegal acts punished by eviction to the homelands, which again depleted the industrial workforce.

With such contradictions between the apartheid laws and economic advance growing, Vorster in 1977 appointed two commissions. The first advised that blacks with skilled jobs and proper housing be accepted as permanent residents in towns, with influx controls enforced against all others. The second commission suggested that job reservation be abolished and black trade unions be recognized and have equal status with white unions, so that skilled black workers would become a *'permanent part of the economy'*.

Granting blacks trade union rights was not so much a concession as a legitimization of what was in any case becoming the status quo. Although black trade unions were not recognized and black strikes were illegal, many industrial managers chose to avoid trouble caused by unofficial or wildcat action by dealing with the unions. At the same time, trade unionism also experienced the familiar characteristic of apartheid rule during this period: on the one hand, reforms conceded as of necessity; on the other was vicious repression and murders of activists.

After the Soweto riots, anti-apartheid groups in Britain and America put pressure on international companies not to operate in South Africa. Promoting and supporting black trade unionism also became an important objective of anti-apartheid forces across the world. There were high-profile campaigns supported by the ANC around British companies with South African subsidiaries, and the British Anti-Apartheid Movement worked hard to build support for economic sanctions.

By 1978, the government had decided to accept the inevitable and turn the skilled black workforce into collaborators in maintaining the system. Blacks essential to the economy would be conceded a share of the nation's wealth and granted residence rights to become a stable workforce, which would act as a buffer between white society and the mass of less skilled blacks, who would remain outside the new system. But there would be no concessions towards political power, and if they were involved in an illegal strike or a riot or were dismissed from work, they would forfeit their residence rights.

———

By the late 1970s, Robben Island was a calmer place: conditions were less brutal, and Mandela had acquired a quiet authority over the younger inmates. A journalist prisoner who arrived in 1980 gave a vivid description of Mandela: '*He walked slowly with a slight stoop and had a lick of gray hair but no paunch, and he was often in deep conversation giving legal or personal advice to other prisoners. He could speak 'fly-taal,' the township slang; he never seemed to be angry and would persuade other prisoners to cool off before they reacted to crises. He was a gentleman through and through*'. The prison officials called him "Mandela" or sometimes "Mr. Mandela", but his fellow prisoners called him by his clan name, Madiba.

The warders were overstretched by the numbers of new inmates so had become more relaxed and their treatment of prisoners was less provocative. Pressures from the Red Cross and elsewhere were having an effect: diet had improved and political prisoners were able to work in the kitchens; Africans were now allowed the same food as Indians and Coloureds.

In early 1977, after two years of a go-slow strike at the lime quarry, the authorities gave in and forced manual work was ended. Warders also proposed turning the politicals' courtyard into a tennis court. The cement was painted green by prisoners with the requisite white lines. Mandela, a sports enthusiast in his younger days, joined in the games more for exercise than love of tennis. The prisoners were now allowed to buy and play their own musical instrument and to stage their own plays; also they could see old movies, including *Cleopatra*, in an improvised cinema. This provoked some comrades to complain that Elizabeth Taylor, who played the part, did not look like an African queen.

But while his colleagues sometimes took several degrees, Mandela had been stopped formally studying for four years, until 1980, and had spent the time discussing, providing legal advice to colleagues, tending his garden and above all reading voraciously: serious novels, political biographies, war memoirs and verse. He also read Afrikaans writers in order better to understand their culture.

Meanwhile, Winnie's banishment to Brandfort had saddened and angered him: '*At least when she was home in Soweto, I could picture her cooking in the kitchen or reading in the lounge; I also could imagine her waking up in the house I knew so well. In Soweto, even if she was banned, there were friends and family nearby*'. In Brandfort she was alone, did not even speak the local language Sesotho, and was in an environment of deep white hostility. It was, after all, the town that had given the architect of apartheid, Hendrik Verwoerd, his separatist vision of Afrikaner dominance.

Winnie had her own inimitable way of handling this nightmare. She saw herself as '*a living symbol of the White man's fear*'. She believed black resistance to be physically '*symbolized by my presence in the kingdom of the Afrikaner, throwing me amongst them*'. So she resolved to give like with like, insisting on using white entrances to the police station and post office. '*There was nothing they could do*', she recalled.

When, as her ban required, she reported weekly to the police station, it was sometimes full of white farmers. '*When I went in there, they automatically made way, not because they were being respectful, but because I had to go in, in order to get out! And the Black people watching this from outside thought it was absolute respect*'. She also went into shops no blacks had ever dared intrude—instead being forced to be served through little windows. '*When I went to the supermarket there were these huge Afrikaans-speaking women. When they saw me they used to run out and stay out until I finished my shopping. But once I started shopping there, the Blacks went in too, and then I would deliberately take an hour to get whatever I needed—even if it was only a piece of soap—and I enjoyed seeing these White women waiting outside*'. This caused such a rumpus that whites petitioned the government to have her removed from Brandfort.

However, Winnie was subject to constant police surveillance and harassment and, in the first two years, was charged over breaching some small regulation or other almost daily. Those living near her were warned not to mix with her. She was banned from meeting more than one person at a time, and when a man tried to sell her a chicken while she was talking to a friend, she was charged with attending an illegal gathering. It was a desolate life in Brandfort for seven years, but she contrived to turn it into her own form of resistance, also refusing to pay her rent, on the grounds that the house was her jail, not her home.

However, Winnie became very ill with a leg infection, and almost died, until by chance her local attorney found her slumped semiconscious on her bed. He rushed her to hospital. But after hours of delay, they refused to operate on her because it was a white hospital. She insisted on being taken back home in a wheelchair and demanded to go to Johannesburg for the necessary urgent operation for which she was exceptionally granted permission the next day. Her treatment lasted six weeks, with security police watching her continuously. The harassment continued when the surgeon said she needed ten days' recovery under observation on crutches. The security police demanded she return immediately to Brandfort, but she refused and went to convalesce at her home in Orlando. Security officers banged on the door, demanding she come out, but she again refused. Only when she was ready did she return to her banishment.

—

Despite all the improvements, conditions on the island remained grim in the late 1970s. The monastic lifestyle, separated from wives, girlfriends and children, caused many psychological strains, as Sisulu explained: '*You long for children more than anything else*'. Ahmed Kathrada told me the same thing when escorting my wife and me around the prison in late 2000. When accompanying Mandela on his visits to Britain, I noticed that children always caught his eye and he cherished them enormously, perhaps as retrospective substitutes for missing his own children and those of others all those long years.

There was a small but very welcome reprieve for Mandela when in 1978 his daughter Zeni married a prince from Swaziland, an independent black statelet where she had been at school. Now a member of a royal family, she had diplomatic privileges and could visit Mandela almost whenever she chose. And because of her status, they could meet together in the same room, on the first occasion with her newborn girl. Mandela waited, nervously: '*It was a truly wondrous moment when they came into the room. I stood up and, when Zeni saw me, she practically tossed her tiny daughter to her husband and ran across the room to embrace me. I had not held my daughter since she was about her own daughter's age*'. As the grandfather, Mandela was given the customary duty of naming the child. He chose Zaziwe (Hope), the name having a special meaning for him: '*For during all my years in prison, hope never left me—and now it never would. I was convinced that this child would be part of a new generation of South Africans for whom apartheid would be a distant memory—that was my dream*'. He held his granddaughter with delight throughout the visit.

In 1981, the younger prisoners, inspired by the IRA's Bobby Sands in Northern Ireland, went on a hunger strike, among other things demanding to be allowed visits from younger children. Mandela joined in the strike, which went on for six days, and eventually some children as young as three were allowed to visit the island.

In a sense being a political prisoner on Robben Island was like a protracted course in a left-wing university. The isolation and shared predicament, with no opportunities for consumerism, moneymaking or rabble-rousing, encouraged idealism and egalitarianism, and developed human sensitivities and communal attitudes. But it encouraged theory rather than practice, so had obvious limitations as a school for practical government, preserving much of the innocence and naïvety of the powerless, with little experience of

the complexities of administration, the drawbacks of state bureaucracies or the dangers of corruption.

Many of the young comrades were ardent Marxists, and in
this questioning university atmosphere Mandela was soon again
challenged, with continuing arguments and debate among the
politicals about Leninist seizures of power and whether communism could work in a modern westernized society such as South
Africa. Eventually, to try to reach a consensus, Kathrada was asked
to write a summary of the arguments. He attempted to dampen the
most revolutionary expectations of the comrades from the battle-
fields, insisting that the South African struggle was quite different
from the revolutions in Eastern Europe, and the ANC and its allies
had never stood for the "Dictatorship of the Proletariat". The document was passed to the other political sections, with a covering
note in Mandela's handwriting saying that it was '*unanimously
approved by the High Organ*'. The island was acquiring a special spirit
of tolerance and discipline. Even though Mandela was the chief
role model, the tolerance and discipline still flourished after he had
left.

There were occasional scares about Mandela's health, but he
was dismissive of minor ailments. When his family doctor visited
him in trying conditions in 1976, he said that Mandela was '*the same
Nel I have known for many years . . . extremely fit, mentally and physically*'. His physique as he approached his sixties was still formidable,
helped by rigorous early morning exercises from 4:30 a.m., when
he always woke.

On July 18, 1978, Mandela celebrated his sixtieth birthday,
which rang around the world. Winnie was not allowed to visit
him, but she was his spokesman, seen as a dedicated wife and long-
suffering activist. '*He's as upright and proud as the day he was arrested*',
she told the *New York Times*. The UN's Special Committee on
Apartheid had called for the occasion to be celebrated, and Winnie
received piles of birthday messages from both governments and
individuals abroad. From Britain, anti-apartheid campaigners sent

ten thousand birthday cards (which were not delivered), and the London *Times* called Mandela '*the colossus of African nationalism*'.

Mandela's lifeline to the outside world remained Winnie. He told her he felt sometimes '*like one who is on the sidelines, who has missed life itself*'. But Winnie could help to connect him. Each year, he counted her letters and visits, now allowed more often, and in 1978 he told her he had had fifteen visits, and fifteen of the forty-three letters were from her. On her visits he asked after old friends, avoiding political news. She outspokenly conveyed his views, as she interpreted them, to the outside world.

Mandela felt more guilty than ever about not being with Winnie and was grateful to people who dared to visit her at Brand-fort. On their wedding anniversary in 1979, he told her, '*You have spent 21 years of your best years rolling about in the treacherous whirlpools of an unfriendly sea*'. On her side, Winnie was struck by Mandela's insights and discipline. By contrast he longed for physical contact, pouring out his emotions in letters quite unlike his measured political messages. But Winnie was now more conscious of the differences in their ages, as she told a journalist in 1983: '*Nelson is 63 now, and I am like a young girl, still longing for the experience of married life*'. Despite his apparent self-sufficiency on the island, Mandela still seemed to depend on Winnie's support, writing to her, '*Had it not been for your visits, wonderful letters and your love I would have fallen apart many years ago*'.

Winnie appeared to have overcome the isolation and hardship of Brandfort—her "*little Siberia*", she called it—with as much self-control as Mandela, and she was making use of her experience as a social worker to build up communal activities such as a crèche, a sewing group and a clinic, assisted by donations that flowed in as journalists and diplomats began to visit her. And she started studying for a degree in social work by correspondence. But as she wrote to her friend, the author Mary Benson in London, '*the empty long days drag on, one like the other . . . the solitude is deadly, the gray match-box shacks, so desolate, simply stare at you*'.

She was, however, not quite the upright and controlled heroine that she seemed to the world, and some friends thought that her ordeals in jail and exile in Brandfort had fundamentally changed her. Unknown to Mandela and away from journalists, Winnie was suddenly erupting into violence and drinking heavily. Her righteous contempt for the police and her international acclaim were combining to give her a sense of being above any law—and within the protection of the ANC she was becoming a bit of a loose cannon.

The children—though suffering less visibly—were another worry to Mandela, and he was preoccupied with their education. When one or the other seemed reluctant or slow to carry out his instructions on studying, he would refuse to let her visit him until she satisfied him that she was studying seriously. When their elder daughter Zeni became engaged, Mandela was concerned that she was only eighteen, was too young for marriage and had not finished high school. He warned his other daughter Zindzi, '*Priority number one is your studies*'.

Zindzi, like Winnie, was spirited, bright and passionate and was more of a problem. When she first visited Mandela in 1976 at the age of sixteen, she was reassured by his warmth. But he was worried about her in Brandfort, away from her friends and alone with her harassed mother. He was solicitous when Zindzi was embarrassed at the prospect of attending Zeni's wedding with bare breasts, following Swazi royal custom, and reassured her. She wanted to become a writer, which pleased him, had begun writing poetry, and in 1978, had published a book of verse, *Black as I Am*, which was awarded a thousand-dollar prize in America.

Mandela loved Zindzi's visits and said, '*You make a wonderful impression on me whenever I see you*'. But he was pained, caught between his stern, fatherly traditionalism and his distance from a teenager suffering from sporadic depression, seeing a psychiatrist and having her studies disrupted. Mandela tried to support her, but her writing had dried up and she backed away from going to university. She had had a daughter by a man from the township and later a son, Gadaffi, by a Rastafarian who would physically assault her. Then she left Winnie in Brandfort and went back to live in the family house in Orlando. Mandela was unhappy that Zindzi was living alone and hoped an elderly aunt might join her, for he knew that the police would continue to harass her.

Mandela also worried about his two eldest children by his first wife Evelyn, son Makgatho and daughter Maki, both of whom had marital problems and were not well educated. He was therefore very relieved when Maki was admitted to Fort Hare, his old university, late in 1978. Mandela gained strength from thinking about his children and his increasing number of grandchildren, but he desperately missed the physical contact with them—continuing to blame himself for being an absent head of family, who had sacrificed them for his political purposes.

Much to his embarrassment, in October 1976 Mandela's own home region, the Transkei, became a so-called independent republic with his nephew, Kaiser Matanzima, elected president and supporting the apartheid government. Another breach developed with Mangosuthu Buthelezi, the Zulu chief, who used to belong to the ANC but who, like Matanzima, had also begun collaborating with apartheid policies as head of the Zulu homeland. Originally with Oliver Tambo's encouragement, Buthelezi had launched his Inkatha organization to mobilize Zulus, adopting the ANC flag and uniform, but he then turned against the ANC, and in July 1980, Tambo announced that Buthelezi was '*on the side of the enemy against the people*'. Mandela still kept in touch with him as an old chiefly friend, but Inkatha remained for the next sixteen years the biggest obstacle to a unified black opposition to apartheid.

However, the churches, which had been cautious in opposing apartheid when Mandela had been jailed, were becoming much more outspoken against it. Desmond Tutu, the irrepressible black cleric, had been appointed dean of Johannesburg by the Anglicans and later became secretary of the Interdenominational South African Council of Churches. He lived near the Mandelas in Soweto, and in April 1980, he said that Mandela was needed *'because he is almost certainly going to be the first Black prime minister'*.

Mandela started reaching out to all the main churches, recalling his own Methodist upbringing and particularly welcoming changes within the original seedbed of apartheid, the Dutch Reformed Church, being delighted by its about-turn in a report that denounced all forms of racial oppression.

He was also receiving more international support: he was awarded the annual Nehru prize for International Understanding in 1979 and in 1980 the Freedom of the City of Glasgow—his letter of thanks ending, *'I have never enjoyed the freedom of the streets, let alone the freedom of the city'*. His letters sounded more and more like the leader of a government in exile waiting to create a new unified nation, and the American vice president Walter Mondale warned Pretoria not to have *"any illusions that the United States will, in the end, intervene to save South Africa."*

The ANC leadership in exile had meanwhile been extending the struggle internationally; regrouping and reorganizing; largely purging its underground of counterespionage agents; establishing military camps, administrative offices and educational institutions in friendly African countries; and organizing infiltration routes. Prior to 1975, the total estimated number of ANC personnel outside South Africa was one thousand; by 1980, it had risen to nine thousand and by 1986 to thirteen thousand (eight thousand under arms with MK).

In March 1980, Mandela saw new hope when the editor of the Johannesburg *Sunday Post*, Percy Qhoboza, launched a petition for his release under the headline "FREE MANDELA." The campaign quickly gained momentum inside South Africa. At a meeting at Wits University twenty years after Sharpeville, his daughter Zindzi explained that the purpose of the petition was *'to say there is an alternative to the inevitable bloodbath'*. There was support from surprising quarters: many whites put "Free Mandela" stickers on their cars, and even the notorious former secret service head General Hendrik van den Bergh now said Mandela should be freed, and he added, '*I challenge anyone to produce one shred of evidence to prove that Mandela was a member of the Communist Party*'. But the hard-line president P. W. Botha (who had succeeded Vorster in 1978) retorted that he would not release the "arch-Marxist".

The Free Mandela campaign reverberated round the world. The UN Security Council joined the call to release him, as the only way to achieve '*meaningful discussion of the future of the country*'. The ANC's sabotage was also beginning to be more effective, avoiding civilian targets and terrorism. In June 1980, their guerrillas put bombs in three major oil-from-coal installations, which lit up the sky fifty miles (80 km) away. Mandela wrote to Tambo that such attacks made the ANC '*undoubtedly a force to be reckoned with*'.

Botha's government tried to stamp out ANC bases outside South Africa, and in January 1981 his forces invaded Mozambique, attacking three buildings in the capital Maputo and killing thirteen ANC people. But MK retaliated, and a bomb exploded in a Port Elizabeth shopping area—in four and half years there had been 112 attacks and explosions.

Nevertheless Botha's anticommunist crusade was gaining support from the neoconservative governments of Margaret Thatcher in London and Ronald Reagan in Washington, together with right-wing organizations in America and Europe, who saw Mandela as the archenemy, with Buthelezi and Botha as champions of free enterprise.

The ANC's hopes of support from independent African states were dashed by failures of their governments, and by coups and countercoups: in more than two decades, twenty-eight African countries had suffered coups d'état, and fifty governments had been overthrown—some by dictators such as Idi Amin in Uganda who ignored human rights. Western businessmen were writing off most of black Africa, while white South Africa depicted itself as the only viable state on the continent. Learning lessons about these problems of democracy to the north, Mandela was determined not to take the same routes.

Free Mandela protest, 1987. Peter Hain and his mother outside South Africa House, Trafalgar Square, London.

We are not calling for his release on humanitarian grounds. We are doing so on political grounds. We are saying that he is our leader. This is the acknowledged leader of the group that most Blacks support, but more than that we are saying he is symbolic because we want all leaders, all political prisoners, released not on humanitarian grounds but on the grounds that this is going to be part of how we build up a climate conducive to negotiation.—DESMOND TUTU

The Cold War continued to distort the politics of Africa, as the Soviet Union supported Marxist regimes while the Americans financed anticommunist leaders. Large areas of recently independent Mozambique were reduced to chaos by incursions of soldiers from the murderous RENAMO rebel group supported by South Africa and the CIA. Angola became a central African battleground for the rival superpowers: the Angolan government brought in Cuban troops to counter the ruthless rebel UNITA army of Jonas Savimbi, financed by the Americans and supported by South African troops.

By March 1982, Mandela had been imprisoned for nearly twenty years, and he had watched the Western world swinging from right to left, and back to right, ending with Reagan and Thatcher. Most Western governments had denounced apartheid but had not given the ANC support—the Swedish government and others in Scandinavia being special exceptions. But the Russians, the East Germans and their allies were training ANC guerrillas and supplying weapons. So, if the ANC continued to look East rather than West, the West had only itself to blame.

Meanwhile, intimidation, abandonment of the rule of law, torture and state terror including assassination remained commonplace inside South Africa. But the tentacles of its police state also spread abroad—in the Cold War environment often tacitly or actively assisted by Western intelligence services in ways that infected and compromised the democratic politics of these countries.

From the late 1960s onward, South African agents were responsible for a series of attacks on the ANC and anti-apartheid organizations across the world. There was harassment and surveillance of activists and burglaries at their headquarters. One of the worst attacks was in March 1982, when the ANC's London office was bombed, its officials narrowly escaping injury or death. Responsibility for this was eventually admitted by the South African intelligence service, which had also murdered one of their former agents, the British-based South African journalist Keith Wallace in London in January 1970. There were many other assassinations including Joe Slovo's wife Ruth First, in August 1982; she had been killed in Maputo when she opened a letter bomb sent by South African agents. In London, I had received a similar letter bomb in June 1972; it had been capable of demolishing our family home and us with it, but a technical fault enabled it to be dismantled by British antiterrorist officers.

Under President Botha, a former defense minister, South Africa was militarized from government downward to the townships.

The responsibility for decision making shifted from the party and the intelligence services under Vorster to the military-security establishment. The Defense Force budget rocketed, and its fighting strength soared. The State Security Council, headed by Botha and including an inner core of cabinet ministers plus the military intelligence and police chiefs, met every two weeks to take the major security-related decisions, which were then ratified by the full cabinet the next day.

However, business leaders convinced Botha that the economy could not expand with apartheid's ideological brakes in place: job reservation had to go to meet the industrial sector's need for skilled manpower, and blacks had to be trained for skilled jobs, which meant upgrading their education and admitting them to whites-only technical institutions and universities. The businessmen also convinced him that a skilled workforce must be allowed to unionize in order to regularize work relations, so black trade unions were granted increased recognition. And the businessmen pointed out that there was no sense in investing in training staff if they had no security of tenure. So this was introduced together with measures to make life in the townships more bearable, such as home ownership and some commercial development. Mortgages were made available for some high-quality housing in black townships to try to create a black middle class, members of which foreign journalists were brought in to interview.

Coopting certain blacks and controlling those who dissented became part of a total strategy by whites who recognized that the old approach of brazen apartheid was not viable socially and was also restrictive economically. At the same time, a better educated and more urbane, prosperous and experienced generation of Afrikaners had emerged at many levels, aware of the impracticability of apartheid, of the manner in which it was thwarting economic advance, and they were embarrassed by its crudity.

However, by identifying with this new Afrikaner middle class, Botha alienated the original constituency of the National Party—the farmers and white workers—and, in the 1981 general election, hard-liners took nearly 30 percent of the Afrikaner vote, and Botha therefore decided to slow down the pace of change. Although he had no intention of dismantling apartheid or undermining white domination and control, he did decide to dump what his ministers described as "outdated" and "unnecessary" apartheid laws, such as the prohibition of mixed-race marriage, all of which provoked such deep discontent among hard-liners that fourteen National Party MPs quit to form a Conservative Party in 1982. This was

extremely significant because it solidified the fracture in Afrikanerdom that had first appeared in the battle inside the National Party
between *verligtes* (enlightened) and *verkramptes* (hard-liners) a decade earlier.

⁓

Opinion surveys in South Africa from 1977 to 1979 showed Winnie to be the most important political activist after the Zulu leader,
Chief Buthelezi, so her banishment did not reduce her national
popularity. In Brandfort she made some friends, not only among
local blacks but also among Afrikaners, including the only local
lawyer, Piet de Waal. Reluctant at first to take her on, he was
warned that he was ethically obliged to represent her because she
could not move out of Brandfort. When she first came to his office,
he complained about the huge crowd massed in her support outside, but he soon began to regard her as a friend, as did his wife
Adele, who came from a well-known Afrikaner family. They
ended up championing her against the police, amazed that a black
woman could be so warm and intelligent.

After de Waal's old friend, the MP Kobie Coetsee, became
minister of justice in 1980, de Waal began pressing him, first to
lift Winnie's bans and then to reconsider Mandela's imprisonment.
Coetsee began to rethink his attitude to Mandela, and as he later
observed, '*you could say that's where the whole process started*'.

In 1980, after a four-year suspension, Mandela was allowed to
resume his legal degree course at London University, and the following year the university's students proposed him as a candidate
for chancellor—he only lost to Princess Anne. That September, the
prisoners were finally allowed to receive South African newspapers,
though these were full of holes cut out by censors.

Mandela had himself learned wider lessons from the "University of Robben Island": he had become more sensitive to other
peoples' insecurities and resentments, and he was no longer the
chiefly autocrat but instead the flexible democrat who could listen
and take note of the majority view. Above all, he was reaching out

to the people he realised he was going to have to negotiate with—
the Afrikaners—and he urged his colleagues to try to understand
their language and their culture. He warned that the "black
Englishmen" with their liberal education (the political prisoners)
could be too readily influenced by the English, *'who have their own
reasons for despising the Afrikaner'*. And in 1978, only two years after
the Soweto uprising, Mandela looked forward to a different future:
*'Today, South Africa has almost three million Afrikaners who will no
longer be oppressors after liberation but a powerful minority of ordinary citizens, whose cooperation and goodwill will be required in the reconstruction
of the country'*.

In February 1981, the Justice Department received a summary
in Afrikaans about Mandela's background and the additional analysis required by the new minister of justice, Coetsee. It stated, *'There
exists no doubt that Mandela commands all the qualities to be the Number
One Black leader in South Africa. His period in prison has caused his
psycho-political posture to increase rather than decrease, and with this he
now has acquired the characteristic prison-charisma of the contemporary liberation leader'*. The document was a remarkably accurate analysis,
which would help to shape the minister's thinking. But at that
time, it gave no answer of what to do with such a formidable
opponent—it would take another nine years before the "Number
One Black leader" was released. But the government was now
locked into a schedule to cement a new order involving some concessions and the cooption of key black groups while retaining
white dominance and privilege.

Then in April 1982, suddenly and without warning or reason,
there was an apparent concession to the ANC. Mandela was visited
in his cell by the island's commanding officer and told to pack his
things for transfer off the island. He, Sisulu, and two other Rivonia
colleagues were taken at dusk to board a ferry for Cape Town and
then into the bleak confines of Pollsmoor Prison, where they were
joined a few months later by Kathrada.

The absence of any explanation was unsettling and disturbing
to Mandela. *'What did it mean?'* he wondered. On the ferry he had

glanced back at the island, which had been his home for nearly twenty years: '*It had become a place where I felt comfortable. I have always found change difficult, and leaving Robben Island, however grim it had been at times, was no exception. I had no idea of what to look forward to*'.

· 7 ·

Victory

Compared with Robben Island, we were in a five-star hotel, Mandela observed about Pollsmoor Prison. The Rivonia prisoners were the only ones on an entire floor, allocated a large room, with—amazing!—separate showers, toilets and basins. The food was much better too.

They were given proper meals, they were allowed more newspapers and periodicals, they could relax on a long rooftop terrace and they enjoyed television, videos and FM radio—things they had never experienced before. Mandela devoured the newspapers, boning up on his cultural know-how and his passion for sport.

Although he had a separate cell for reading and writing, he felt disoriented and more isolated, missing the camaraderie, arguments and even the wildness of the island, where they had been much closer to nature than in Pollsmoor, a cold concrete warren of dark corridors. Mandela's strict regime of rising at 4:30 a.m. for an hour's exercise also irritated his four comrades, woken up each morning as he pounded round the large cell.

Winnie came to see him soon after his arrival and was impressed by the prison and by the more humane visiting conditions. She and Mandela could see and hear each other properly, through clear glass and loud amplifiers. But she too felt he was worse off, removed from his many friends in the wider island community. He complained about the cold, damp cell and the lack of any view and said he had not seen a blade of grass since arriving at Pollsmoor.

The relative comfort could not hide their anxiety that they had been separated off from the others *'to cut off the head of the ANC on the island by removing its leadership'*, as Mandela feared.

But outside things were on the move. In 1983, the Botha government put forward new constitutional proposals approved by a whites-only referendum for a tri-cameral Parliament with separate houses for whites, Coloureds and Indians in which the white chamber was able to outvote the other two at all times. Black "political rights" were to be limited to allowing them to elect local authorities in the townships.

In response, a huge rally was called near Cape Town to boycott the elections. More than four hundred organizations sent delegates, and about ten thousand people of all races attended and launched the United Democratic Front (UDF), naming Mandela as a patron.

The UDF proved an especially powerful force because it was so difficult for the government to act against. The government sponsored organizations had committees, and many had premises, but the UDF had neither—nor did it have property or formal leaders for the police to seize. When UDF patrons were detained, the UDF continued in limbo until its member groups next decided to activate it. The only policy it adopted was a watered-down version of the ANC's Freedom Charter, so bland that not even the government could object to it. Effectively it was acting as a surrogate ANC, as many of its members privately acknowledged.

Meanwhile, in May 1983, the ANC's military wing, MK, exploded a car bomb outside the air force headquarters in Pretoria, killing nineteen and injuring two hundred—both black and white—which shocked Mandela: *'The killing of civilians was a tragic accident, and I felt a profound horror at the death toll. But disturbed as I*

*was at these casualties, I knew that such accidents were an inevitable conse-
quence of the decision to embark on a military struggle'*. But as its founder
commander he thoroughly approved of a subsequent daring mission that shook the white community, when later that year MK
blew up a section of the Koeberg nuclear power station near Cape
Town, delaying its commissioning by eighteen months.

—

President P. W. Botha's foreign policy was much more aggressive,
offering economic opportunities to adjacent black states that cooperated and ruthlessly destabilizing those that did not. The latter
included armed strikes into countries by both land and air, killing
local civilians and arming and supporting insurgent rebel guerrillas
such as RENAMO in Mozambique and UNITA in Angola,
encouraging hugely destructive civil wars.

This strategy eventually reduced Mozambique to economic
ruin and forced it in late 1983 to sign the Nkomati Accord, in
which it agreed to exclude ANC bases in return for the South Africans withdrawing all support from RENAMO (which in fact they
did not). But in Angola the policy failed and the South Africans
overreached themselves, provoking Cuba into a massive buildup of
its military assistance to the ruling MPLA government, an ANC
ally. In 1988, for the first time, the Cuban forces were sent south
to engage a South African column that was trying to take the
MPLA's main southern stronghold of Cuito Cuanavale. The column encountered heavy resistance and was surrounded. As South
Africa tried to supply and relieve its force from the air, it found that
it had lost its accustomed air superiority, and the beleaguered column began to suffer heavy casualties. Mandela was thrilled, for this
was a major blow: never before had the powerful white state been
defeated militarily in Africa. South Africa then agreed to accept
withdrawal from Angola and independence for Namibia in
exchange for Cuban withdrawal but at a cost to the ANC of
removal of its bases from Angola.

—

The UDF successfully organized against the new constitution in the most sustained and vigorous political campaign that black South Africa had ever been able to run. It ensured a derisory turnout of Coloureds and Indians in the elections in August 1984 and an almost total boycott of the council elections in black townships. Opinion polls showed that the ANC was hugely popular among blacks, despite being banned for a quarter of a century.

Black anger continued to fuel the UDF's massive support, and in September 1984 violence erupted against dreadful conditions in the townships. A typically brutal response from the police provoked rioting to spread across the country, involving a much wider range of groups than in Soweto in 1976, which had been a largely youth revolution. This time, the UDF spanned generations and interest groups—trade unionists, educators, students, politicians, exiled ANC leaders and former Black Consciousness leaders were all members. White liberals, students and radicals were also involved. A variety of strategies were employed: consumer and rent boycotts, school boycotts, strikes and stay-aways, rallies, protest demonstrations and a mix of street confrontation with public and private negotiation.

The 1984 troubles were more intense and lasted longer than previous ones, raging for three years and resulting in more than three thousand deaths, some thirty thousand detentions and untold damage to property and the national economy. The army was mobilized and a state of emergency declared on two occasions to control it. But this was only partially achieved. The central aim of the unrest was to make the townships ungovernable. However, this was not a plan decided upon by ANC strategists in exile, let alone leaders like Mandela in prison. Although the ANC remained influential, there was a spontaneous reaction from the grassroots in the townships.

Residents stopped paying rents to the government agencies and instead new UDF-inspired street or area committees collected fees. They also conscripted their supporters and decided when to call strikes or boycotts. Black police were driven out of some townships, and the committees organized their own crime prevention forces and set up people's courts.

In the Port Elizabeth townships, the UDF attained such control that it was issuing hawkers' licenses. White businessmen negotiated safe passage for their vehicles with the UDF, and its leader in the area, Mkhuseli Jack, was in such demand that he carried a beeper so that he could be contacted easily. When the police detained Jack and his colleagues, the businessmen pleaded for their release so they could negotiate an end to the boycott—and the police complied. In a small harbinger of things to come, business came before apartheid's crumbling politics.

The pressures were intensifying, and in January 1985, Botha announced to Parliament that Mandela would be released in return for a promise not to take action that would lead to his rearrest, tantamount to him renouncing the ANC.

I cannot and will not give an undertaking at a time when I and you, the people, are not free. Your freedom and mine cannot be separated.

Mandela saw this offer as a positive sign of coming real negotiations, which he craved, but he disdainfully rejected it. How could he leave on the basis of renouncing all that he had gone to prison for and continued steadfastly to believe in? In a powerful reply, read to a UDF rally in Soweto in February by his daughter Zindzi—a speaker similar to her charismatic mother—Mandela defiantly rejected the offer. He was open to proper negotiations but would only come out when he and his people could be free. He reaffirmed his full support for the ANC and the UDF to an ecstatic reception, not least because it was the first time Mandela's words were able to be heard legally in public for more than twenty years. Botha responded privately to his trusted and equally tough justice and security minister, Kobie Coetsee, '*You know, we have painted ourselves into a corner. Can you get us out?*'

Frustration increased, and the violence intensified. MK freedom fighters infiltrated townships and trained groups of "comrades" (as the young activists were known). In February 1985, organized street fighters with bursts of AK-47 automatic rifle fire scattered police.

Soon, the unrest swelled to local civil wars as the "comrades" fought pro-government black "vigilantes". Though the leaders tried to impose restraint, there was inevitably much savagery by the "comrades", especially against those considered to be collaborators, and the gruesome practice of "necklacing" began—placing a tire filled with gasoline around the neck of the black victim and setting it alight.

Ferocious police violence and widespread detentions of activists continued. But President Botha was caught between a rock and a hard place, especially when the United States became the first major Western state to initiate effective economic sanctions against South Africa, as black Americans started insisting on that as the price of their vote. Pressures were being mobilized worldwide in support of the rising level of internal struggle.

For some time, South Africa had experienced difficulty raising foreign loans and had been forced to take out high-interest, short-term loans to raise much-needed foreign capital. By August 1985, two-thirds of South Africa's huge foreign debt was in loans that could be called up at any time—and a hard-line speech by Botha caused them to be, led by American banks, followed by Britain, Germany and Switzerland. The South African rand soon fell by a third and reached an all-time low.

Introduced at long last, these loan sanctions started to create precisely the impact that had led Mandela and anti-apartheid forces the world over to advocate them for decades. South Africa was unable to meet the repayments; foreign exchange and development capital were denied, and white living standards plunged.

The apartheid government's options were running out. And when Nelson Mandela was taken from Pollsmoor in November 1985 for hospital surgery on an enlarged prostate gland, Botha and the minister of justice, Coetsee, decided it was time to meet him secretly. It was a cathartic moment for the irascible, iron-strong Botha—"the crocodile" as he was called. For he was sending a secret emissary to see if the feared "communist terrorist" prisoner—the man terrified Afrikaners imagined might eat their babies—could help save their country. For Mandela, it was the opportunity for the dialogue he had sought for decades. If it went wrong, both men had so much to lose.

But the instant Coetsee walked into Mandela's hospital room, he was charmed. Instead of the intimidating, bearded freedom fighter of popular image, there was a polite, welcoming gentleman, thin and a bit weak after his operation. '*He was a natural, and I realized that from the moment I set eyes upon him. He was a born leader. And he was affable. He was obviously well liked by the hospital personnel and yet he was respected, even though they knew that he was a prisoner. And he was clearly in command of his surroundings*'. They talked animatedly about Afrikaner history—Coetsee surprised by Mandela's sympathetic knowledge—and family matters, including a chance encounter with Winnie on a plane, which had followed her lawyer's earlier representations to him. Coetsee saw it as opening a new door: '*to talk, rather than to fight*'.

He reported back to Botha, and they agreed that Mandela would not be discharged to rejoin his four old comrades but instead be allocated a cell on his own, from where meetings could be held in secret. Though unhappy to be separated, Mandela concluded it offered advantages, especially that he could now pursue the negotiations he had wanted in freedom, as he later explained to his fellow prisoners. They were uncertain, but Mandela was clear: '*I knew that my colleagues would condemn my proposal, and that would kill my initiative, even before it was born. There are times when a leader must move out ahead of the flock*'.

Thereafter, Coetsee had several more secret meetings with him in a guest house in the prison grounds, and one meeting where he was suddenly driven out to the minister's house. But Mandela, isolated and taking risks, was also anxious to maintain trust with the leadership outside and was able secretly to communicate the substance of these meetings to Oliver Tambo, who reported back in February 1986 that the exiled ANC leaders had confidence in Mandela's ability to handle the situation and that he should carry on with their full support.

Meanwhile, there were violent clashes in black townships, notably Crossroads outside Cape Town, and open rifts surfaced between reformists and hard-liners in Botha's government. Pressure was also rising through the Commonwealth for tough sanctions, and a delegation was dispatched to South Africa, the Commonwealth Eminent Persons Group (EPG) in May 1986, headed by Malcolm Fraser, the Australian prime minister, and General Obasanjo of Nigeria. The EPG drew up a '*possible negotiating concept*', which they put to both the ANC and the government. This included the release of Nelson Mandela and other political prisoners, unbanning the ANC and PAC, withdrawing the army from the townships and allowing free assembly and political activity, with the ANC agreeing to suspend its guerrilla activities and entering into negotiations.

The ANC indicated it might respond positively but awaited the government's reaction before finally deciding. From Pollsmoor Prison Mandela indicated his personal approval.

But the hard-liners won at a cabinet meeting on May 13; the EPG initiative was rejected, and the government dispatched military raids against "ANC bases" in Zimbabwe, Botswana and Zambia. The so-called base in Zambia, bombed by South African planes, was in fact a United Nations camp full of Angolan and Namibian refugees.

In June, another state of emergency was declared, placing the country under martial law. The reforms were dropped, and under Coetsee the government launched the total onslaught that the hard-liners had been calling for. Organizations were banned; open-air gatherings, prohibited; and the police and military moved into the townships to detain thirty thousand, including eight thousand children and three thousand women—more than in the entire twenty-five years since Sharpeville. Vigilante bands—formed from township residents with cause to resent the "comrades" excesses—were armed and turned loose on the more radical townships. Activists' homes were burnt; and the offices of anti-apartheid organizations, bombed. (Despite denials at the time, it was confirmed in the 1990s that this vigilante strategy was authorized at the highest level of the government.) By late 1987, ninety-seven townships were under military occupation and the rebellion was virtually over. But though badly disrupted organizationally, the resistance continued to retain the support of the black community.

From inside Pollsmoor, Mandela viewed it all with a combination of deep frustration at the terrible violence and hope that his infant dialogue might bear fruit. His prisoner existence had become somewhat bizarre as ministers were evidently preparing him for life on the outside. He was without notice taken for a drive around the city and the beautiful Cape peninsular: '*It was absolutely riveting to watch the simple activities of people out in the world: old men sitting in the sun, women doing their shopping, people walking dogs. I felt like a tourist in a strange and remarkable land*'. This was to be the first of many such excursions, and however enjoyable they undoubtedly were, Mandela sensed there was an ulterior purpose: '*Perhaps to get me so used to the pleasures of small freedoms that I might be willing to compromise in order to have complete freedom*'.

In the run-up to his seventieth birthday in July 1988, the cry went up around the world to "Free Mandela". The campaign had been carefully planned by the anti-apartheid groups throughout the world. Mandela's international stature was by now immense, and the signals that the government had been courting him only reinforced his influence. He had become a symbol both of the oppression of apartheid and of the alternative to it. The climax of the campaign was a spectacular "Free Mandela" concert at Wembley Stadium in London organized by the British Anti-Apartheid Movement and attended by one hundred thousand, who saw some of the world's leading pop groups perform, along with hundreds of millions watching on television across the globe, enhancing Mandela's stature as a household name.

An all-star line-up graced the stage at Wembley for the "Free Nelson Mandela" concert. One of the biggest television events in history, it was watched by more than six hundred million viewers worldwide. Image ID: GA8CJ4

Winnie had become another symbol of the struggle for freedom, widely admired internationally for her courage and determination in raising a young family while her husband remained in prison. When her house in Brandfort was bombed and burned down in 1986, she defied her ban and returned to her home in Soweto. The government did not move against her, and tragically she increasingly became a law unto herself. She refused to work in a collective way with the UDF and instead surrounded herself with a group of young men called the Mandela United Football Club, who accompanied her as bodyguards. Within months, they were terrorizing the township and, late in 1988, kidnapped four young men from a church refuge, interrogating and assaulting them. A week later, one of them—Stompie Moeketsi Seipei, a popular teenage activist—was found dead, and the "trainer" of the "football team" was found guilty of his murder. In exile, the ANC criticized Winnie's "judgement", and in February 1989 the leaders of the UDF declared that Mrs. Mandela had abused '*the trust and confidence of the community*'.

—

Mandela in Pollsmoor had meanwhile been meeting not just Coetsee but also other senior government figures including, highly significantly, Neil Barnard, the head of the infamous National Intelligence Service, who later explained that he disagreed with others (including military and police leaders) who thought '*we had to fight it out in some way or another*'. He believed that '*a political settlement was the only answer to the problems of this country*'.

On Botha's instruction he met Mandela for the first time in May 1988 at an office in Pollsmoor. As with Coetsee, they quickly formed a rapport, Barnard insisting that wearing overalls and boots was unacceptable for these meetings; Mandela had to be '*clothed in such a way that it serves his dignity and pride as a human being*'. He also instructed that meetings had to be outside the prison buildings, beginning at the commanding officer's home. There, they shared dinner and wine and talked for hours about the complexities of ending apartheid peacefully, as the "total war" the state had unleashed on black resistance raged in the country outside. It was as if apartheid's rulers were playing both ends off against the middle, as Mandela was only too shrewdly aware. But instead of angrily confronting Barnard over the merciless repression outside (which he knew would be pointlessly counterproductive and only drive the government figures talking to him back into their shells), he pressed ahead with the dialogue. He couldn't control terrible events outside, but from inside he might be able to shape the future.

Then in December 1988, again without notice, he was told that he was being transferred out of Pollsmoor to a spacious modern bungalow with a swimming pool in the grounds of Victor Verster Prison, in the heart of the Cape winelands, an hour's drive north of the city. The prisons minister Coetsee was his first visitor, armed with a housewarming case of wine, both men fully conscious of, as Mandela later put it, '*the irony of a jailer bringing his prisoner a gift*'. Coetsee explained that this would be his last home before being set free, and it was intended to give him a comfortable environment for private discussion. While enjoying his new freedom—to walk, to swim to sleep, and to wake up as he pleased—Mandela '*never forgot that it was a gilded cage*'.

Soon he was meeting his four comrades brought over to his new home from Pollsmoor and drafting with their help a memorandum to President Botha. It offered a way of meeting the demands made of the ANC by the government in order to end '*a South Africa split into two hostile camps . . . slaughtering one another*''. Majority rule and internal peace, he argued, "*are like the two sides of a single coin*'.

That July, he entertained nearly his entire family—from Winnie to his grandchildren—at his seventy-first birthday party, for the first time ever. His white cook and house help prepared a veritable feast: '*The only pain was the knowledge that I had missed such occasions for so many years*'. At his new home, he also met other key ANC and UDF leaders and continued his discussions with, among others, Neil Barnard, who told him, '*Mr. Mandela, governing a country is a tough job. It's not like, with a lot of respect, sitting in a London hotel . . . and talking about government*', thus aiming a barb at exiled ANC leaders. Barnard became '*captivated*' by Mandela: '*He has this strange charisma. . . . So, yes, there was in our minds, looking from an intelligence perspective, never the slightest doubt. This is the man—if you cannot find a settlement with him, any settlement will be out*'.

In parallel, there were secret meetings abroad between prominent Nationalists and the ANC from 1986 to 1990, helping to break down the stereotypes that each believed about the other. In 1986, the ANC director of information Thabo Mbeki, attending a Ford Foundation Conference in New York, met the chairman of the Broederbond (Brotherhood), the Afrikaner secret society that had devised the apartheid ideology and was the think tank for government strategy after 1948. Other Broederbond members and government advisers, including the brother of Botha's successor, F. W. de Klerk, Wimpie, became involved in a series of clandestine meetings in London.

International business was anxious to promote some sort of rapprochement and to set up an important series of exploratory meetings at the request of the ANC. There were report-backs via Neil Barnard to President Botha and from Wimpie de Klerk to his brother. Thabo Mbeki and Jacob Zuma, the key ANC figures, were aware of these report-back arrangements from the beginning. For the Afrikaners, the meetings demolished the demonized image of the ANC built up by years of propaganda, while the ANC leaders in exile became sensitive to white anxieties, particularly to Afrikaner fears of survival under black majority rule. There was now a tentative basis for further dialogue. There was also an extraordinary meeting in October 1988 in Zimbabwe between the legendary white father figure of South African rugby, Danie Craven, and a top ANC delegation led by Thabo Mbeki. They discussed the desperation of whites to have the sports boycott lifted and agreed in principle that the ANC would press for an end to the ban if rugby were reorganized on a fully nonracial basis.

—

After six months of meetings with Barnard, Mandela demanded to see his boss, delayed for some months after Botha had had a stroke. On July 5, 1989, Mandela was taken to meet him secretly in the president's official residence in Cape Town; he was kitted out in the new suit and tie he had requested of the prison commander. While they waited, Barnard bent down to tie Mandela's shoe laces properly, with Coetsee also in attendance, both nervous about how it might go. But despite a remarkably warm meeting, Botha was not forthcoming on the question of negotiation.

Botha had been furiously resisting calls that he resign because of ill health. But cabinet ministers, led by F. W. de Klerk, now installed as National Party leader, insisted. Just weeks after meeting Mandela, he was deposed, and after a general election in September 1989, F. W. de Klerk became president. Despite having shown no visible reformist signs, he promised a '*new South Africa, a totally changed South Africa*'.

De Klerk had been regarded as a conservative and said that his change to reformer was not a question of morality but of practical politics—part of a gradual realisation within the National Party that apartheid was unworkable. He always refused to apologize for apartheid, maintaining that it was merely a policy that "didn't work" and that his predecessors had been dedicated, sincere people. But his real emancipation from apartheid ideology had begun with his election as National Party leader in February 1989, after Botha's stroke. As party leader he made several trips abroad—most unusual for a National Party leader—where the heads of state that he met all emphasised the need for South Africa to change.

Also crucial was the new international climate of an end to the Cold War, following dramatic reforms by the Soviet leader, Mikhail Gorbachev; these comprised his internal glasnost and his external rapprochement with the West. This meant that neither Washington nor Moscow any longer had a strategic interest in perpetuating a regional conflict in southern Africa, which was instead becoming more of a headache. For Washington, white South Africa's role as a "bulwark against communism" had become obsolete. For Moscow, there were more pressing domestic demands for funds that had gone to support liberation groups like the ANC.

And contrary to what apartheid apologists from Margaret Thatcher and Ronald Reagan downward had maintained, the imposition of financial and other sanctions had bitten deeply. The chorus of white complaints about falling living standards was becoming more insistent, even hysterical. A final decisive factor was resistance to white rule. Anti-apartheid activists abroad were operating in a more conducive climate than ever, and boycotts were proving effective, from sports to arms.

Within South Africa, the ANC was increasingly powerful.

There was growing internal resistance orchestrated by the UDF and the new Mass Democratic Movement formed in 1989 out of an alliance between the UDF and the black trade union congress, COSATU. The ANC's military wing, MK, had the ability to strike and wound. The trade unions were also a major threat, the 1987 miners strike having shown the economy could be paralyzed if subject to a general strike, which could be sparked off at almost any time.

Events began to accelerate at a breathless pace two weeks after de Klerk's election in September 1989. First he ordered the release of one of the leading ANC figures, Govan Mbeki, from Robben Island. Shortly afterward, Walter Sisulu and seven other top ANC political prisoners were released, and eighty thousand people gathered in a football stadium in Johannesburg to welcome them. During December, Mandela had three meetings with de Klerk.

Speculation about his own release was rife—though those of us involved in the bitter decades of struggle could hardly believe that the end was beckoning. During a secret visit to make a British television documentary in December 1989, I had a unique opportunity to make sense of the tumultuous changes about to be unleashed in the country. Among ANC activists operating through the UDF and the Mass Democratic Movement there was a mood of confidence I had not expected. People who had just emerged from long years of detention spoke with determined optimism about their plans for the future and their belief in the inevitability of white rule ending in a negotiated solution.

For its part, white authority seemed rather punch drunk, unsure about the new ground rules. For instance, the ANC was still banned and the press was still prohibited from carrying Nelson Mandela's picture, but the ANC's colors were worn or displayed openly. Some protests were being permitted, provided they received prior police permission and conformed to tight restrictions. Others were still repressed—as when protesters against a rebel cricket tour from England were attacked by police at Johannesburg airport and when four thousand people marching for better education were dispersed with water cannon in Cape Town. Despite having been agreed in advance, protests around the rebel tour quickly degenerated into violent clashes with police. At the same time, morale among white police and security forces had collapsed due to government legitimization of protest and defiance and the exposure of state-sponsored "death squads".

The striking thing about going back after twenty-three years was the extent to which the government was being forced to change, not out of desire but out of necessity. Time did seem to be running out for whites-only rule. There seemed a realisation that they no longer had sufficient bullets. But I also sensed that whites were losing their political will to govern by the old methods of ruthlessly maintaining their privileges by force and where appropriate outright terror.

Perhaps it was a little premature to seek parallels with the still fresh tumult in Eastern Europe following Gorbachev's reforms and the collapse of the Soviet bloc. But there was a sniff of the same demise of an old order, which in East Berlin a few months earlier allowed people to pour buoyantly into security police buildings that only days before they had passed by terrified. The armed might of South Africa's police state was still intact and white political power, still immense. But there comes a psychological moment when that doesn't count any more.

Events were moving very quickly. Nelson Mandela—hugely popular at grassroots level in the townships and tactically sophisticated—was being transformed among many white media commentators from feared enemy to national hero. But this was also probably the last opportunity for a peaceful transition. If it failed, the balance of power within the resistance movement would shift downward to younger, more militant elements doubtful about the prospects for successful negotiations. Also, if it failed, the world would turn its back as the country toppled into the abyss.

⁓

On February 2, 1990, President de Klerk opened the first session of the new Parliament and made good his promise of a "new South

Africa". He surprised everyone by announcing the unbanning of the ANC, PAC and other outlawed organizations, and he gave notice of the impending release of Mandela and hundreds of other political prisoners. He declared his readiness to enter into negotiations with all of them to work out a new constitution in which everyone would enjoy equal rights. The impact of the speech was breathtaking. Listening to it broadcast live in London, I found the implications took some time to sink in. Across the world, anti-apartheid supporters phoned each other or chatted excitedly as they gathered in front of televisions or radios in disbelief. But there was no going back—either for whites or for anti-apartheid forces. An entirely new political agenda had opened up.

The release of Nelson Mandela himself followed, on February 11. It had been announced in advance, indeed orchestrated, with the government carefully releasing the first photograph of Mandela for decades, meeting de Klerk in the president's rooms. It revealed not the big freedom fighter in the prime of his life, which for years had appeared the world over, but a slim, dignified, old African statesman with a smile of destiny that hovered somewhere between the benign and the all-knowing.

However, all the careful choreography nearly came unstuck as, once again without any notice, Mandela was told by de Klerk at a meeting in the president's residence that he would be released the following day. Mandela objected, explaining that his family and the ANC would have no time to prepare. He wanted a week's notice and also insisted upon walking out of Victor Verster Prison, rather than being flown to Johannesburg as the government had planned. After some toing and froing, they settled on a compromise: he would walk out of Victor Verster, but because the world's press had already been informed, it would have to be the next day. '*It was a tense moment and, at the time, neither of us saw any irony in a prisoner asking not to be released and his jailer attempting to release him*', Mandela remarked.

Few who watched live television on February 11, 1990, will ever forget the image of the world's most famous political prisoner, kept out of sight for more than a quarter of a century, walking to freedom through the gates in the prison fence; it was one of those defining moments in history that many ordinary onlookers will remember forever, recalling exactly where they were and what they were doing. Millions of viewers in his country and across the world wept openly. With his wife Winnie by his side, Mandela walked towards the massed ranks of TV cameras and thousands of well-wishers.

Except for his obvious humility and humanity, he looked almost regal, a giant among his people, though a little bemused by the sheer numbers of media and thousands of supporters. Instinctively raising his right fist in the ANC salute, the crowd roared: '*I had not been able to do that for 27 years, and it gave me a surge of strength and joy. As I finally walked through those gates I felt—even at the age of 71—that my life was beginning anew. My 10,000 days of imprisonment were at last over*'. Yet he would not have been human without admitting something else: '*Yes, I was angry. And I was a little afraid. After all, I'd not been free in so long. But when I felt that anger well up inside of me I realized that if I hated them after I got outside that gate then they would still have me. I wanted to be free so I let it go.*'

He then climbed into a car in an ANC cavalcade for the thirty-five-mile (56 km) drive to Cape Town along a road lined with smiling, waving crowds of all races. The release had, however, gone more than two hours past its advertised time because Winnie had been late at her hairdressers, and Mandela reprimanded her, angry at keeping everyone waiting. By the time they reached Cape Town's City Hall, he was five hours late, and the crowd, which had waited in the hot sun, was understandably restless and tense. His speech was rather limp, but it did not matter. From a balcony, with the eager upturned faces filling the Grand Parade below, he raised his fist in the ANC salute and cried out, '*Amandla! Amandla! Mayibuye iAfrika!*' (Power! Power! Let Africa return). '*Friends, comrades and fellow South Africans, I greet you all in the name of peace, democracy and freedom for all. I stand here before you not as a prophet but as a humble servant of you, the people'.*

President de Klerk and his subordinates watched all this with some nervousness. How would Mandela handle his all too obviously visible popular power? Would he stick to his promises to preach a new common purpose for all? They need not have worried. Early the next morning, in the garden of Archbishop Desmond Tutu's official residence, he charmed more than two hundred local and international journalists. Uniquely for that hard-bitten bunch, they gave him a spontaneous ovation at the end. He was masterful, especially as he had never handled a live television press conference, commonplace for leading politicians in the modern era. His appeal was directly to the anxious white population outside, calling President de Klerk (an apartheid veteran with twenty years of harsh governing under his belt) *'a man of integrity'*, acknowledging by name his kinder jailers and indicating in the clearest way that he had no bitterness, that he was instead focused upon building a new future for all South Africans.

The Mandelas then flew to Johannesburg and drove to his small house in Orlando West and on to Soweto's football stadium, where he spoke to a crowd of 85,000 in the stands and about 120,000 outside. The exhilarating mood surrounding his every appearance captivated not just black South Africa but also a world watching almost continuous live broadcasts.

So the most turbulent era in South Africa's turbulent history had come to an optimistic end: Mandela and other leaders freed, the ANC and other outlawed organizations unbanned and an Afrikaner leader at last prepared to negotiate with the 75 percent of South Africans who had never enjoyed democratic rights in their own country. But although the new South Africa beckoned, its birth pangs were still fraught with anguish and, as it transpired, more violence than at any time in apartheid's bitter history.

—

Talks between the South African government and the ANC—previously ad hoc and exploratory—now began in earnest. There was much to settle before constitutional negotiations could start, and in May 1990 temporary indemnities against prosecution for having violated the security laws were issued to all the ANC members who were to attend, and they were flown from exile to Cape Town.

Then, in August, Mandela announced the unilateral suspension of the ANC's armed struggle. Although there was private criticism within the ANC and among anti-apartheid activists of this suspension, Mandela's supreme authority in the movement and his skill easily carried the day. He knew that for a peaceful transition to succeed there had to be give and take, and he and his fellow ANC negotiators progressively squeezed further concessions out of the de Klerk government.

After these preliminary agreements, the black parties set about the problems of returning exiles, released prisoners and local activists reacclimatizing themselves and integrating themselves into cohesive political movements. Mandela knew that for the ANC especially the major challenge was to change from the culture and habits of an underground revolutionary movement to those of a political party about to engage in conventional politics.

His already huge international profile was built up with a punishing series of tours abroad. There was a one-hundred-thousand-strong rock concert at London's Wembley Stadium to welcome him as a free leader. He appeared on stage between acts to deliver a powerful appeal for support and received a rapturous reception. In New York's Yankee sports stadium, he addressed another bumper crowd after the city had granted him a ticker-tape welcome reserved for only a select few. He took America by storm, dominating the media and being feted by its top politicians; his visit preceded that of de Klerk whose appearance went almost unnoticed. There was no doubt that the world, like black South Africans, was receiving Mandela as the country's leader-designate and awaited his imprimatur before sanctions could be lifted and normal relations established.

This was very significant because, although de Klerk acted

with courage and vision during this period, he was not about to hand over control. When he spoke of a "new South Africa", he was not really envisaging majority rule. Rather, he wanted "power sharing" between what he called "a nation of minorities"—the ten black chiefdoms, the two white groups and the Indians (for him the Afrikaans-speaking Coloured people would be regarded as Afrikaners). His strategy was to build an anti-ANC alliance with Chief Mangosuthu Buthelezi's Inkatha movement, with other Bantustan leaders, and also with the Coloured and Indian minorities, which he assumed would share the whites' fear of black majority rule. He wanted to allow time for Mandela to go from being the messianic figure he was at the time of his release to just another fallible politician, pressured by the constraints of the situation into losing credibility with his mass of followers. And de Klerk wanted Western sympathy to shift from the ANC to his government, as the world responded to his boldness, lifted sanctions and shrank from the ANC's commitment to socialism. So he was still intent on hanging onto power.

As a result, the negotiations over the new constitution were fraught and remained deadlocked for six months by disagreement over preconditions and format, until Mandela brokered a solution in January 1991. But it was not until October 1991 that a preparatory meeting of all the participating parties took place.

Around Mandela raged the tensions of the negotiations and the bitter birth pangs of the new emerging politics. On international visits he would be pushed from pillar to post, with thousands of people—all important in some way—anxious to meet him. Amid all this, I met him for the first time in May 1991. As everyone else who was privileged to be introduced to Mandela confirmed, he had a gentle sense of authority that was unique. He was relaxed, dignified, courteous to a fault, and somehow above the ordinary mortals who pressed his flesh. He had the stillness of a man of destiny at the eye of a political storm.

When the first plenary session of the negotiating conference (called CODESA) opened nearly two years after Mandela's release,

Durban, July 1991. Mandela celebrates his freedom at his first ANC conference since his 27-year imprisonment. Image ID: BR0664

de Klerk attacked the ANC. Mandela responded angrily, accusing him of being '*less than frank*' and describing him as '*the head of an illegitimate, discredited, minority regime*'. De Klerk was visibly rattled, the exchange a portent of things to come.

—

Under his public persona, however, Mandela was tortured by disappointment and grief over Winnie. As his prison letters showed, he idolized her. But once released everything altered. She had changed—and fundamentally. Mixed up in the murky murder of the young activist Stompie, living an oddly luxurious lifestyle with numerous younger lovers, she was not trusted by the ANC, either with funds or for her political impetuosity.

As Mandela bestrode the outside world, she appeared alongside as his beautiful and articulate consort, attendant to his interests, with huge credibility among young ANC militants and a populist charisma. In private, however, their relationship barely existed. Maybe it never could have sustained the twenty-seven years apart, in view of the twenty-year age gap and the appalling emotional and physical suffering visited upon her, week after week, by the security police. Mandela had changed too. Perhaps because he was only able to survive and thrive in prison by building emotional barriers around him, friends and relatives noticed after his release how his incredible public warmth and individual charm contrasted with a certain emptiness behind locked doors in private. Maybe he had only so much to give.

To his daughters, Mandela was both loving and yet distant. Winnie later complained, '*He has never returned, even emotionally. He can no longer relate to his family as a family. He relates to the struggle that has been his lifetime*'. Mandela saw it differently, however, and said of Winnie, '*She married a man who soon left her. That man became a myth; and then the myth returned home and proved to be a man after all*'. Mandela turned up in court in February 1991 when she was tried and found guilty of complicity in the death of Stompie—the judge damning her as '*a calm, composed, deliberate and unblushing liar*'. However, her six-year prison sentence was set aside on appeal.

In April 1992, Mandela called a press conference and, flanked by his old comrades Sisulu and Tambo, painfully announced their separation: '*I part from my wife with no recriminations. I embrace her with all the love and affection I have nursed for her inside and outside prison from the moment I first met her*'. At their divorce hearing in 1996, he revealed that '*not once has she ever entered my bedroom whilst I was awake*'. He was, he said, '*the loneliest man*'.

While together in their separation, in their togetherness they began to discover how apart they had become.—FATIMA MEER, friend and biographer

In March 1992, de Klerk called a whites-only referendum to seek approval for the negotiations. Mandela urged supporters not to disrupt the referendum and called on white ANC supporters to vote for approval. Once more in apartheid's history, sport played a key political role. The ANC had encouraged the newly formed United Cricket Board to reestablish South Africa's international links. For the first time in a quarter of a century, South Africa participated in a cricket venture abroad, the Cricket World Cup staged in Australia. Live television and saturation press coverage enthralled the white population starved for so long by isolation. And the government, in a timetable of carefully orchestrated political advertisements and TV broadcasts, used pictures from the World Cup to urge a "yes" vote as the only means of keeping such international sports participation. Where sport had been used as a stick to force change, now it was a carrot. De Klerk won with a two-thirds majority on an 85 percent turnout. However, he used this mandate not simply to press ahead with the changes but also to toughen the National Party's negotiating stance at CODESA.

The second session, CODESA 2, began in May 1992 with the ANC trying to hurry things along and the National Party trying to draw them out. The expectant masses in the townships grew restive at the government's intransigence and delaying tactics, at a time when they were being subjected to increased political violence by vigilantes from Inkatha, Chief Buthelezi's Zulu party having excluded itself from the negotiating process. Living in migrant workers' hostels, these vigilantes were supported (and in many cases orchestrated) by the police. Although Mandela and other ANC leaders continued to express optimism, the process of transition was in crisis.

It was only in March 1994 that the Goldstone report revealed a terror campaign systematically organized by a "third force", which reached right to the top of the security services, the police, the defense forces and even into the cabinet. Based at Vlakplaas, a farm west of Pretoria, it was responsible for the attacks on black commuter trains, for township massacres launched from Inkatha hostels and for supplying arms to Inkatha. It had also trained Inkatha members in sabotage and assassination. It established death squads in the police, which murdered ANC members in Kwa-Zulu/Natal. And it was responsible for the deaths of civil rights activists and prominent ANC members throughout the country.

Given the scale of the third force's activity, it is hard to believe de Klerk was ignorant of its existence since some of his closest allies were involved. He and the government as a whole were still determined to destroy or at least cripple the ANC. That way they might cling onto power even in the democratized state that was now the price whites accepted had to be paid for international approval and internal stability. Overwhelming evidence emerged that hit squads and destabilization, together with collusion between the security forces and Inkatha, actually intensified after de Klerk's negotiations with the ANC began. Political assassinations of prominent local figures jumped about tenfold per annum from the 1980s to reach fully ninety-seven in 1992. Violence in Natal also reached new heights after Mandela's release, as Inkatha warriors attacked ANC communities, killing and maiming.

Mandela decided to respond by launching a campaign of

"rolling mass action"—a series of strikes, boycotts and street demonstrations, which began on June 16, 1992, the anniversary of the
1976 Soweto uprising. Soon afterward he announced the ANC's
formal withdrawal from negotiations, listing fourteen demands the
government must meet before talks could resume, the most critical
an end to '*the regime's campaign of terror*' against the ANC. The government rejected these demands, and what was described as a "war
of memoranda" ensued.

There were terrible clashes in the "self-governing" homelands, where the ANC was prohibited by local black rulers from
organizing itself, while de Klerk was meanwhile pushing ahead
building his anti-ANC alliances in each one. The worst came in the
Ciskei Bantustan on September 7, 1992, when a crowd of eighty
thousand led by the ANC marched on the Ciskei capital Bisho, just
outside King William's Town in the Eastern Cape. As they tried to
bypass a line of black Ciskei soldiers officered by white South Africans, the soldiers opened fire. Twenty-eight marchers were killed
and more than two hundred wounded. Captured on television, the
shock of Bisho reverberated through the nation. Mandela offered a
new way forward, and de Klerk reacted positively by inviting Mandela to join him at a summit meeting to find a way to end the violence.

In the government camp, the group of young Afrikaners faced
the reality that their futures and career prospects lay in what would
inevitably be a nonracial South Africa. The necessity to come to
terms with the ANC seemed much more realistic than trying to
build an anti-ANC alliance with Buthelezi's Inkatha (which was in
any case losing support to the ANC among Zulus). And in the
ANC, a similar change was taking place, with some of the moder-
ates exploring how they could bridge the gap between power sharing and majority rule, thereby strengthening Mandela's hand.

By March 1993, the negotiations were back on track and now
injected with a new common purpose. Yet still the old reactionary
underbelly of apartheid fought back. Chris Hani, the general secretary of the Communist Party and a famous ANC guerrilla leader

and hero to the militant young "comrades", was shot dead at his Johannesburg home by a white gunman, a leading member of the Conservative Party, who was later arrested and found guilty of the murder. This was an explosive moment, capable of plunging the country back into carnage and terror. Only Mandela could defuse it, and he did so by issuing a moving appeal on national television: '*A White man full of prejudice and hate . . . committed a deed so foul that our whole nation now teeters on the brink of disaster. But a White woman, of Afrikaner origin [Hani's neighbor who reported the murder], risked her life so that we may know, and bring to justice, the assassin*'.

There were further signs of extremist white resistance to a democratic transition. On June 25, as delegates gathered for their morning session of the constitutional conference, a noisy mob of three thousand Afrikaners, some in the uniform of the extremist Afrikaner Weerstandsbeweging (AWB [Afrikaner Resistance Movement]), crashed a military vehicle through the plate-glass front and rampaged through the building, vandalizing it and jostling black delegates. The police guarding the building did nothing. A further shock occurred on July 25 at St. James's Church in Cape Town, which was packed with more than a thousand white worshippers, when five masked blacks stormed in, opened fire on the congregation and fled, leaving twelve dead and fifty-six injured. Nobody acknowledged responsibility, and it was suspected that it might again have been the work of the "third force".

In September 1993, a Transitional Executive Council (TEC) was set up to work in tandem with the government to prepare for a free and fair general election on April 27, 1994. The negotiations survived all the provocations, with the last clause of the constitution being adopted on November 18, 1993. It underpinned majority rule with guaranteed minority party rights, including cabinet seats for the first five years in a Government of National Unity (GNU), and protected the jobs of white soldiers, police and civil servants.

But white extremists and Afrikaner fundamentalists remained

hostile. They included the Volksfront (People's Front) led by General Constand Viljoen, which demanded a separate Afrikaner *volkstaat* (people's state). Mandela's vital leadership once more came into play as he met with Viljoen, and drawing on all the insights into Afrikanerdom he had first developed on Robben Island, he sought to reassure him that Afrikaner interests could be protected.

Then, in March 1994, there was a dramatic turning point that broke the back of right-wing Afrikaner resistance to the coming election and split the common white right front into squabbling factions again. It had been agreed to restore South African citizenship to all blacks living in the Bantustans, which would be absorbed back into South Africa on election day on April 27. But early in March, the autocratic president of Bophuthatswana, Lucas Mangope, announced that he would not participate in the election and that his government would retain the independence granted it in 1977 under the apartheid system. Within days, the territory's civil servants and police began striking, demanding that their wages and pensions be paid out in advance of April 27. As anarchy spread, Mangope appealed to his allies in the Volksfront for help, stipulating that there must be no AWB men among the Volksfront forces.

But the Nazi-like AWB leader Eugene Terre'Blanche, a member of the Volksfront executive, immediately ordered the AWB members of his commando units to head for Bophuthatswana. The AWB men, some six hundred strong, came in their farm trucks and cars with hunting rifles, shotguns and pistols, rampaging through, yelling racial abuse at the locals and taking pot shots at people, killing and wounding.

They so outraged the Bophuthatswana Defense Force that it mutinied, and its soldiers drove through the town shouting ANC slogans and firing on the AWB raiders. Some of the AWB rabble lost their way and roared along, still shooting at bystanders; one car burst firing through a police roadblock and was halted by police gunfire. Two wounded men fell out of the car onto the road, begging for medical help and mercy. But with TV cameras recording the event, a young black policeman angrily screamed at them,

'*Who do you think you are? What are you doing in my country?*' Minutes later, they were both shot dead.

For the white rightists, this traumatic experience, shown nationwide on South African TV, had a cathartic impact and blew away the ancient myth that the white race, with its superior arms and training, could always dominate the blacks. It also destroyed the folklore that whites would always fight to the last to preserve their supremacy. Here they had indeed fought and lost—their most fanatical militarists actually gunned down by a black, live on television.

After the debacle Bophuthatswana came into the fold, and Constand Viljoen, with only ten minutes to go to the midnight deadline, registered a new white Afrikaner party, the Freedom Front (FF), to participate in the election. Although Buthelezi's Inkatha party was still resistant, Mandela appealed to him: '*I will go down on my knees to beg those who want to drag our country into bloodshed*', he told a rally in Durban—Buthelezi's backyard. Eventually, only a week before the first of the three election days, the Inkatha leader finally agreed to take part.

So South Africa was ready at last for her first ever nonracial, one-person-one-vote election. The dream that had sustained generations of struggle, but that seemed so impossible, was at last in sight.

At every opportunity, I said all South Africans must now unite and join hands and say we are one country, one nation, one people, marching together into the future.

· 8 ·

President

$\mathcal{T}$he sun shone all day long as if to salute the bubbling joy of history in the making on Wednesday April 27, 1994, when Nelson Mandela voted for the first time in his life. Characteristically, he joked when the waiting media posse asked him who he was voting for: '*You know I have been agonizing over that choice all morning!*'

The day before I had gone as British parliamentary observer to his final election press conference, where he presided with his usual saintly, benevolent authority, patient but clear, grave though occasionally witty. Afterward, I found myself unexpectedly alone in an anteroom with Mandela as he rested. We chatted amiably for around ten minutes. He was tranquility personified, even oddly downbeat: '*Peter, I suppose I should be jumping for joy. But I just feel a stillness. There is so much responsibility, so much to do*'. Everybody—from the media to his personal staff—treated him as something extremely precious: the seventy-five-year-old president in waiting, who held the whole country's future in his hands.

Next morning, to meet my observer duties, I arrived half an hour early at our first polling station in Orlando, originally home to Walter Sisulu and Mandela, the gold-mine dumps looming in the early mist.

There were thousands already queuing up, their mood calm and expectant. More were streaming in out of the morning haze,

151

Ohlange High School, Inanda, April 27, 1994. Mandela voting for the very first time, aged 75. Image ID: A16GAP.

and as the sun lifted, the queue disappeared out of sight. On official business, my black driver was able to jump the queues and vote first. As he put his ballot form in the box, he turned to catch my eye, smiling, part triumphant, part astonished—before leaving the polling station with a broad grin and punching the air in excitement. Hardly able to accept that, in middle age, he had actually been allowed to vote for the very first time, he had been worried in case his ballot paper might be snatched away at the last minute.

It was the same for hundreds of thousands around us in Soweto and millions across the country, many of whom queued quietly in the burning heat for many hours to exercise the democratic rights they had so long and so mercilessly been denied. I saw an old woman—perhaps in her nineties—led shuffling away with a smile of eternity gracing her weathered face as young men bounced confidently out of the polling station in their trainers, saluting their

Pretoria, May 10, 1994. From political prisoner to president: Mandela is sworn in. Corbis, Corbis Saba/Louise Gubb.

friends. After all those years, all the bitterness, the killings, the violence and the lives wasted away in prison, here, unbelievably, it was actually happening: constitutional apartheid being exorcised.

After logistical delays, the results were announced on May 6, and the ANC won a landslide 63 percent and a big majority in Parliament with F. W. de Klerk's National Party on just 20 percent. Many in the ANC were disappointed because the ANC had fallen short of the two-thirds needed to be able to write the new and final constitution on its own. But Mandela was relieved: the need to get multiparty consensus would deliver what he wanted—a "South African constitution" not an "ANC constitution", as he put it, reflecting the spirit in which he would lead the new Government of National Unity (GNU) announced on May 11. It included ministerial portfolios for the ANC's main opponents, including as a deputy president de Klerk, who earlier had graciously conceded defeat after three centuries of white minority rule.

'*I saw my mission as one of preaching national reconciliation*', explained Mandela. '*I knew that many people, particularly the minorities—Whites, Coloureds and Indians—would be feeling anxious, and I wanted them to feel secure*'.

—

South Africa's first black president was inaugurated on May 10, 1994, at Pretoria, South Africa's administrative capital. There, at the Union Buildings, the grand neoclassical seat of government, which lords it over the city from its hillside perch, VIP dignitaries sat in the sun, while on the broad lawns below a multiracial crowd of more than fifty thousand waited expectantly.

'*In the presence of those assembled here, and in full realization of the high calling, I assume as president in the service of the Republic of South Africa I, Nelson Rolihlahla Mandela, do hereby swear to be faithful to the Republic of South Africa . . .*'.

The four thousand assembled VIPs—heads of state, visiting ministers, royals and others—rose spontaneously to their feet for an ovation in a moment of genuine emotion. And as the cheering died away, across the city came the roar of helicopter gunships, jet fighters in acrobatic flights trailing the new South Africa flag, swooping in to salute their first ever black commander in chief.

—

Mandela in his mid-70s became president four years after being released from prison. He was without any experience of '*elections, of parliamentary practice and of state administration*' (as he put it), yet he was suddenly thrown into the '*immense responsibility of running a highly developed country*'. This was nothing new in Africa: from Kwame Nkrumah in Ghana in 1960 to Robert Mugabe in Zimbabwe in 1980, all had been in the same position and had faced unfamiliar problems. Mandela saw himself in the African tradition and was determined to show that Africans could govern effectively: '*Yes, Africans, with their supposed venality and incompetence*', he said pointedly. '*Never, never and never again shall it be that this beautiful land will again experience the oppression of one by another and suffer the indignity of being the skunk of the world'.*

But he did know that he was taking over a much more developed, industrialized and complicated country than any other in Africa, in which it would be some time before black South Africans could govern without support from white managers, technicians and professionals. He was aware Mozambique had been devastated by a sudden exodus of whites on independence, with its president, Samora Machel, warning fellow Africans to avoid the same fate.

South Africa was much more dependent on white expertise because its state education system had always been separated into white and black schools, with Hendrik Verwoerd, the minister responsible, stating in 1955, '*There is no place for the Bantu in the European community above the level of certain forms of labor*', which in effect meant that state schools would train Africans only for menial work. So Mandela took over an otherwise modern country in which a huge proportion of the population lacked modern skills—a fundamental legacy of apartheid left to future generations to overcome. His challenge, therefore, was pacifying the white elite without alienating the black masses.

Mandela soon occupied his presidency as if he had been born to it. He liked to recall how he arrived at the president's office in the Union Buildings in Pretoria and found no staff around. He summoned a senior civil servant and asked him to assemble the staff next day. The following morning, he shook their hands, reminded them a new government had taken over and assured them that no one would be thrown onto the streets. Soon he established excellent relations with the white Afrikaner staff, who became totally loyal to the genial old man who remembered their names and families. Prickly at first, the Afrikaner protection officers he inherited soon said they would happily die for him.

Zelda la Grange, of impeccable Afrikaner stock, was a young typist in the president's office when she bumped into Mandela in August 1994 and started crying—an embarrassing outburst of '*that feeling of guilt that all Afrikaners carry with them*', she later explained.

He consoled her, talking in Afrikaans, and after a year she became his effective gatekeeper and constant touring companion, going with him into retirement. Indefatigable and intensely loyal, with a shrewd integrity, she remained indispensable to the international icon.

Mandela took over the president's office in Cape Town where, when still a prisoner, he had first met P. W. Botha in 1989. Allowing de Klerk to remain in the official presidential residence, he occupied an elegant Cape Dutch mansion. He still often got up at 4:30 a.m., did his exercises, made his own bed as he had done on Robben Island and walked around the grounds before breakfast.

He amazed the staff and servants by shaking hands and chatting with all of them, including the gardeners. De Klerk noted that '*he had an exceptional ability to make everyone with whom he came in contact feel special*'. In Pretoria, he gave a new intimacy to the official presidential residence, Libertas, which was renamed Mahlamba Ndlopfu (Washing of the elephant). However, he still lived in his house in Houghton in Johannesburg, where he could remain a private person, albeit a lonely one, now as president more cut off from old friendships. The greater his fame, the more his isolation. As his daughter Zindzi said, '*The sad thing is that nobody realises that my father is very lonely*'. He was much older than all his colleagues—Oliver Tambo was dead, and Sisulu was outside the cabinet.

Winnie had played no part in his social life since they separated in April 1992, but she still caused political problems. She had become an ANC MP at the election, and Mandela appointed her deputy minister of arts, but she soon became involved in financial scandals. Mandela did nothing until she accused the ANC of being preoccupied with appeasing whites. After he insisted she apologize, Winnie reluctantly signed a formal apology, yet almost immediately she told an African crowd, '*Your struggle seems much worse than before*', and he was forced to dismiss her.

He sought relaxation with unpolitical people at weekends and relished the undemanding company of show business personalities or the rich—not realising he was more of a celebrity than any of them. But he kept his distance from the values of the rich; when he was staying in a luxurious enclave in the Bahamas, surrounded by white expatriates, he gave a talk to pupils at a nearby black school, which appalled the white community by its militancy.

He was most obviously at home in his newly built house at Qunu in the Transkei, a long, single-level dwelling, with wide arches and a wide, low roof, set back from the main road from the main town Umtata, and surrounded by a garden and trees. It looked across the scenic Transkei landscape, to a few mud-walled, grass-thatched huts, so redolent of his childhood. '*This is really home, where my roots are*', he explained.

Mandela remained a star performer who played all the parts: the African chief, the Western president, the sportsman, the philosopher and the jiver with the "Madiba shuffle". In his first months as president he enjoyed a brilliant honeymoon, particularly with white South Africans, to whom this tolerant old man was a wondrous relief and dispelled white nightmares of a black revolution. He publicly met and forgave his vindictive old prosecutor, Percy Yutar, and went for tea with the aged wife of the ruthless apartheid architect, Hendrik Verwoerd. Among whites, the fear slowly ebbed as Mandela mutated from devil to hero. On a family visit over Christmas 1994, with my parents returning for the first time, I could feel the new South Africa starting tentatively to bed down, buoyed by an infectious optimism from whites and blacks alike—though they too were caught by the same sense of wondering whether it was actually true.

Every time Nelson Mandela walks into a room we all feel a little bigger. We all want to stand up; we all want to cheer; because we'd like to be him on our best day.—BILL CLINTON

Mandela's physique and stamina amazed his physicians, including his old family doctor Nthatho Motlana, who kept urging him to slow down. He still had trouble with his eyes, and flashlights were forbidden when photographing him. His knee had not recovered from a fall on Robben Island but could not safely be operated on; eventually he needed help to walk upstairs. Sometimes he suffered from exhaustion and his doctors insisted on total rest. But he recuperated quickly, used his long flights in the presidential plane as a rest and appeared unaffected by jet lag. The doctors agreed that his energy and vitality were like those of a man twenty years younger.

From the start, Mandela set the strategy and vision of the government. But he was a big-picture president, determining the style and tone of the new country he led. For the delivery of government he relied heavily on his first deputy president, Thabo Mbeki, twenty-five years his junior and the leading exile, who had a difficult task. Where Mandela was given credit for triumphs, Mbeki took the blame for mistakes. While Mandela led from the front, Mbeki worked from behind, schooled by his mentor Tambo. Inscrutably puffing his pipe, Mbeki would fix and bargain behind the scenes through a small group of confidants, the troubleshooter picking up the pieces and filling the gaps. He faced a particular challenge from black militants who saw the revolution betrayed. Younger ANC leaders, including Mbeki, knew they would soon have to make reforms that would offend the whites.

Parliament's most important task was to approve a new constitution, which was hammered out by the ANC's brilliant preelection negotiator Cyril Ramaphosa. It was put to Parliament and ratified in October 1996. The real battles to transform the country were waged within government departments, and here the substructure of the existing officialdom was hard to budge. The ANC tried to neutralize those white civil servants who were in post and actively obstructive, but this took time, as did the training of qualified black administrators to take their place. The lack of black middle managers, especially in the provincial governments, was the greatest obstacle to the transformation of government, and it was here that the true cost of educational apartheid also showed itself.

There were compromises in every ministry, but the main one was in finance. Huge outflows of capital in the previous eighteen months had left reserves dangerously low. Ministers learned to live within strict budgets—the interest payments on debts incurred by previous apartheid regimes consumed one-fifth of the entire national budget. Slowly, but surely, a reputation for good economic management was built, albeit at the cost of reining in ANC ambitions and hopes. By the end of Mandela's five-year presidency, a course had been set that would begin to see the transformation of the economy from a white basket case into a black success story.

Some plans soon proved overambitious: the target of a million new houses in five years could not be reached, and the promise of more jobs proved hollow as new technologies required fewer employees and put a premium on skills that most blacks still lacked. Nationalization was no longer seen as an option for creating jobs.

This was a bitter pill not only for ANC ministers but also for Afrikaners whose governments had provided thousands of jobs for them in overmanned nationalized industries and public bureaucracies—their own version of "affirmative action".

Mandela's government was closely watched by the world's businessmen and diplomats for signs of corruption similar to those that had occurred in many ex-colonial African states. The Afrikaner governments had been notorious for taking bribes, and the ANC needed to clean up both the networks of bribes and the treats from Pretoria and from the Bantustan governments. White entrepreneurs were also now dangling bribes in front of politicians to acquire business footholds.

Mandela himself lived simply and gave one-third of his salary to the Children's Fund, which was his special charity. But MPs were under fire for accepting big salary increases, causing Archbishop Desmond Tutu to quip, '*The government stopped the gravy train long enough to get on it*'. A few months later, Mandela announced a cut in the salaries of MPs and of the president.

By the end of his first year, white South Africans were complaining about the crime wave, the falling currency, corruption scandals and upheavals in hospitals and schools (no longer for whites only). Most blacks took a more positive view: the rural poor saw the extension of primary health care and the arrival of water taps, and in the cities the burgeoning black middle class saw expanding opportunities in industry and commerce.

—

On June 24, 1995, Mandela awoke at 4:30 a.m. as usual and confessed to being more tense than at almost any time in his life—more than awaiting the verdict at the Rivonia trial or the day he became president. That afternoon was the Rugby World Cup final between the Springboks and the New Zealanders not too far from his home in Johannesburg. In a masterstroke, he turned up to greet the teams in a Springbok cap and jersey, uniting the whole nation in a famous rugby victory. The crowd—mostly diehard Afrikaners—rose to cheer him, chanting, "Nelson! Nelson! Nelson!" Almost the entire nation of forty-three million was glued to its television sets. Blacks, who had traditionally supported Springbok opponents, found themselves cheering "their" team. Even a year into his government, sport was still as potent a force for change as it had always been in the rise and fall of apartheid. Mandela, a sports fan himself, knew all along that there was one thing that could unite whites and blacks: both were mad about sport and obsessed with winning.

I never imagined it would have such an impact. All that I was doing was continuing my work of mobilizing all South Africans to support rugby and to influence the Afrikaners, especially towards nation-building.

He remained adamant about the necessity to conciliate Afrikaners, and he considered forgiveness an aspect of power, establishing a moral supremacy that reminded everyone that the balance had shifted. He was eloquent in support of a free press. But within South Africa he pointed to the overwhelming influence of white editors and owners, and said, '*With the exception of the Sowetan, the senior editorial staff of all South Africa's daily newspapers are cast from the same racial mold: White, male, from a middle-class background and sharing a very similar life experience*'. He accused the media of double standards, defending their own freedom of speech while regarding any government counterattack as an attempt to suppress them, although he remained personally averse to censoring anything.

The collaboration of Mandela and de Klerk in the GNU was a historic achievement, and the GNU was working better than most members had expected, but the two leaders were never easy together. The new constitution, which was agreed in May 1996, did not provide for the National Party to stay sharing power at the executive level until, as they had wanted, the end of the second Parliament in 2004; so de Klerk announced the withdrawal of his party from the government.

Within a few months, the once-invincible National Party was in disarray: one member had resigned to cofound his own party, and de Klerk soon retired from politics. He had hoped that Mangosuthu Buthelezi and his Inkatha would follow him out of the government, but Buthelezi told him he would not leave unless his party instructed him to, and he stayed on as minister of the interior. When Mandela was out of the country at the same time as Mbeki, he shrewdly appointed Buthelezi as acting president.

Mandela believed that, with the exception of the Holocaust, '*there is no evil that has been so condemned by the whole world as apartheid*' and that the ANC had to find a way to forgive without forgetting. The result was his launch in February 1996 of the Truth and Reconciliation Commission (TRC), which had originated as part of the hard bargain of the "negotiated revolution". De Klerk and his security forces had constantly insisted on a general amnesty, but the ANC would not allow the apartheid regime '*to grant amnesty to itself*'. After fierce arguments, it was eventually agreed that the commission would grant individual amnesties on condition that the perpetrators revealed the truth and could prove that their actions had been politically motivated. The TRC would have quasi-judicial powers to grant individual amnesties with subpoena powers and hearings in public. But applicants for amnesty would have to come out with the whole truth.

Mandela appointed Archbishop Tutu as chairman, who turned the hearings into a mixture of trial, confession and morality play, with an African dimension. At the TRC's opening dedication in February 1996 in Cape Town's Anglican cathedral, Mandela gave a subdued address, repeating that *'we can forgive but we can never forget'*, and promised the commission would be free from all political interference. Over the next two years the hearings, which were played out on TV, radio and the press, revealed more horrific stories than most people, including Mandela, had imagined, as both perpetrators and victims described the cold-blooded details of torture and assassinations. The ANC admitted that twenty-two members had been executed in camps abroad for mutiny, betrayal, rape and murder, but most of the evidence was inevitably about awful, bloodcurdling atrocities committed by the apartheid forces. When summoned to give evidence, Winnie was belligerent, refusing to apologize for the murder of Stompie Moeketsi Seipei and the criminality that had surrounded her in the late 1980s. Tutu was able to drag reluctantly from her only that some *'things had gone horribly wrong'*.

The commission completed its report in October 1998, and it aroused furious reactions from both sides. De Klerk, who was accused of covering up bombings, appealed to the High Court, and the TRC's judgements on him were blacked out in the printed report. The ANC, having seen only part of the report, demanded a special hearing, was refused and went to court against Mandela's advice to try to stop publication. The application was dismissed, confirming the seriousness of the ANC's blunder, for which Mbeki was primarily responsible. Mandela continued to be totally supportive of the TRC regardless of what it uncovered. In the aftermath, there was much discussion about granting a general amnesty, but he insisted that amnesties should be given only on an individual basis.

He's got so much to teach us about forgiveness. It isn't about being soft-headed and kind-hearted and essentially weak. Mandela found that forgiveness was a strategy for survival. Because he found a forgiving heart under the most adverse circumstances, because he learnt to hate the apartheid cause without hating White South Africans, he had space left inside to learn and grow and become great. In the process he freed not only Black South Africans but he freed White South Africans too.—BILL CLINTON

Mandela had decided to give up his presidency of the ANC by the ANC annual conference in December 1997, while remaining president until the end of his five-year term in 1999. He made his decision public in August that year, and it was clear that Mbeki would succeed him as president of the ANC, though he would have been happier with Cyril Ramaphosa, and he was alarmed that Winnie might stand for the deputy presidency.

The conference was held in Mafikeng, when Mandela presided over his party for the last time. He emphasised that his withdrawal from office would not mean a sudden change in leadership and said that Thabo Mbeki was already de facto president of the country.

He warned them of the dangers of corruption and greed, and against the "careerism" of politicians who use their positions to make money; he told the ANC to work to attract white voters; he criticized white businessmen for the slow pace of transformation and black empowerment; and he blamed the media for neglecting black viewpoints.

The speech was not in keeping with Mandela's usual statesman-like surveys, and it attracted considerable media criticism, both in South Africa and overseas. But it was not a policy state-ment; it was an analysis of the problems of over three years of gov-ernment and a rallying call for the election in sixteen months' time.

The following day Mbeki was confirmed unopposed as the next president of the ANC. Winnie was nominated from the hall for the deputy presidency, seconded by only twenty delegates and received only 127 votes from the 3,500 delegates. Jacob Zuma, the popular candidate, won.

Mbeki was a quite different kind of leader—astute and worldly but an introvert from a bookish background, without deep rural roots—and one who played his cards close to his chest. Some Africans complained that he had spent too long in England, and he obviously felt the need to show himself as a true African because of his cosmopolitan past and overseas friendships. He kept his distance from white businessmen and journalists and took many advisers from Black Consciousness networks. Indian and white colleagues feared he would play the race card and that the multiracial vision of South Africa would fade.

Meanwhile Mandela's private loneliness had been changing. In July 1990, on a visit to Mozambique, he had met Graça Machel. She was the widow of Mozambique president Samora Machel, who had died in a mysterious air crash in 1986, and the Mandelas had sent a joint message of condolence.

Two years later, after he had separated from Winnie, they met again when Graça came to Cape Town to receive an honorary doc-torate. Thereafter, he saw her whenever he could. Tambo had been custodian to Machel's six children, and after Machel died, Mandela took over that responsibility.

Graça was then forty-six (twenty-seven years younger than Mandela), vivacious with a strong character but not domineering like Winnie. She had received a Methodist Scholarship to Lisbon University, where she became politically active against the Portu-guese colonial power. After her degree she trained as a fighter for the FRELIMO liberation movement in Tanzania and met Samora Machel, whose wife had died. FRELIMO became the government when Mozambique gained its independence in 1975, and Graça became minister of education, aged twenty-nine. Soon afterward, she married Machel, looking after his six children. She was now in a young country that was being devastated by the rebel army RENAMO and the mass exodus of whites, and destabilized by the South African apartheid government, which was widely suspected of being responsible for her husband's death.

Graça became involved with children's welfare, which linked her to Mandela's Children's Fund. From mid-1995, she began increasingly to be seen with Mandela at functions and by 1997 had clearly become the president's consort. Mandela was visibly enchanted by Graça, by her warmth, grace and love of children.

Their friendship became public knowledge, and in September 1996 he was photographed on a Sunday afternoon walking near his Houghton home with his arm around her. He had earlier proposed to her, but she was concerned about her obligations to her family and her country, and eventually they agreed that she would spend two weeks every month with him in Houghton. This arrangement occasioned some criticism, not least from Tutu, and they eventually married on Mandela's eightieth birthday—July 18, 1998—to the delight of all his many friends and supporters.

In his last months as president, with Graça by his side, Mandela covered much of the world to say goodbye, and with Graça, Mandela's friends saw a more relaxed and carefree man, who was personally happy at last.

In February 1999, Mandela gave his last annual speech to Parliament on the state of the nation. Many whites had been relieved that their lifestyles were largely unaffected by the political upheaval of 1994, but they could no longer belong to a quite separate society with its own privileges and rules, an appendage of the rich world of the West; they were now part of a developing country in a state of continuous change, like Brazil or Mexico, exposed to all the problems and hazards of a growing and impoverished population streaming into the cities. Mandela's government had faced a series of crises that seemed like caricatures of the developing world, in the fields of race, immigration, finance, health and education.

It was fortunate for the whole white community that the ANC was not only wedded to democracy but also highly sophisticated. For the South African miracle is not just about the historic uniqueness of the white elite ceding the privileges of power; it is also about the extraordinary generosity shown by blacks when assuming it. Here Mandela was crucial as an inspirational leader of historic stature who was big enough to keep his eye on building a new future rather than looking to an old past. And underneath him the ANC had a long-developed culture of leaders and activists who were on the one hand astute in the art of negotiation and compromise and on the other clear-sighted enough about objectives to maintain legitimacy with their grassroots in conditions of high volatility.

Mandela's life story was central to his country's story. Brought up with tales of the humiliation of his own chiefdom, he had lived through the rise and fall of apartheid. As president, he had seen the persistence of apartheid attitudes and the many strongholds of racism that remained. But he had refounded a nation, stamping it with the concept of racial tolerance and cooperation as firmly as his predecessors had stamped it with intolerance and segregation. Yet, as he said at the end of his presidential farewell speech to Parliament on March 29, 1999, '*The long walk continues*'.

· 9 ·

Mandela Magic

*I*t was a bright summer's day at the majestic castle in the capital of Wales, Cardiff, in June 1998. The packed crowd was expectant, the VIPs were lined up to greet a most important guest to receive the Freedom of the City and I was the government minister tasked with introducing him.

But Nelson Mandela ignored my guiding arm on his elbow and stopped when a group of primary schoolchildren caught his attention. As the queue of VIPs waited, sweltering in the unusually hot weather, he began conducting the children to sing "Twinkle, Twinkle Little Star".

Cardiff that day experienced a vintage Mandela performance, singing and dancing with the children, and meeting my father again for the first time since they had been together in South Africa in the anti-apartheid struggle forty years before. *'Are you still causing trouble?'* he asked.

A couple of years before, he had abandoned suits and usually wore the smart-casual, bright, loose-fitting, Hawaiian-type shirts first introduced to him in Indonesia; these became his hallmark, known as "Madiba shirts", and he wore one on that day.

Two years later, I again escorted him, this time to see Prime Minister Tony Blair before Mandela's address to the annual confer-ence of the Labour Party. He asked me his usual question: *'How's the family?'* On hearing my mother was in hospital with a fractured femur, he stopped immediately. *'I must speak to her'*, he said. Out came my mobile, and when she answered from her bed, she was greeted with *'Hullo. Nelson Mandela here, do you remember me?'* Meanwhile, the prime minister was kept waiting.

Of all the public figures and international statesmen I have met—and there have been many—none had Mandela's capacity for engaging self-deprecation, wit and common touch. In retirement on a visit to London we talked and he said that his wife Graça would be along later—*'She is much more important than me'*. When he had announced in August 1997 that he would not serve a second term as president, he downplayed his role: *'Many of my colleagues are head and shoulders above me in almost every respect. Rather than being an asset, I'm more of a decoration'*. Another saying of his was to claim: *'I am just a country boy'*.

Mandela's capacity for mischief was also very evident when, a few weeks after my marriage in 2003, I introduced my wife Elizabeth to him. *'Is this your girlfriend?'* he asked. When I replied, *'No, she's my wife'*, he chuckled: *'So she caught you then?'* And when Elizabeth exclaimed indignantly that she'd taken a lot of persuading, he laughed, *'That's what they all say, Peter, but they trap you in the end!'* By then she realised he was teasing her, and we all ended up laughing and talking together. He apologized for not coming to the wedding, having instead sent a message. *'But perhaps I will be able to come the next time!'*

On his ninetieth birthday in 2008, he had a request to phone Buckingham Palace and speak to the queen. *'Hullo Elizabeth, how's the Duke?'* he said; perhaps only he could have got away with such disregard for royal decorum. When his wife Graca reprimanded him, he retorted: *'Well she calls me Nelson'*. She also tried to stop him drinking at the party as he hilariously hid his glass of champagne from her.

A defense lawyer at the Rivonia trial, Joel (subsequently Lord) Joffe, said, *'When I last met him in his home in Johannesburg, he was sitting on a low sofa. Being quite frail, he struggled to rise. I said, "Madiba, please do not get up for me", and he, with a mischievous twinkle in his eyes, replied as he rose, "I always stand up for a member of the House of Lords".'*

It was not just his towering moral stature, his courage and his capacity to inspire that endeared Nelson Mandela to so many. Despite being one of the world's most prominent statesmen— perhaps the most revered—he retained his extraordinary humanity. When he was with you, you had all his attention. When he greeted you, his eyes never wandered, even though you were surrounded by more important people, whether you were a mere child, a hotel porter, a cleaner, a waiter or a junior staff member. And he never forgot a friend.

This ordinariness combined with extraordinariness is not Mandela's sole uniqueness. His capacity for forgiveness is what made him the absolutely critical figure, first during secret negotiations with the Afrikaner Nationalist government in the late 1980s from prison and then after his release.

He was acutely concerned at how close South Africa had come to civil war—Buthelezi's Zulus and Afrikaner extremists even at the eleventh hour very nearly defied the carefully negotiated settlement.

In July 1996, Mandela was still reminding the ANC at a private gathering of struggle veterans, '*You mustn't compromise your principles, but you mustn't humiliate the opposition. No one is more dangerous than one who is humiliated*'. Nobody else could have delivered such a healing presidency in such a bitterly divided country with so much vicious nastiness in its history still lurking in the shadows of the transition and for many years afterward.

A cathartic piece of Mandela magic was in 1995 when, dressed in the very Springbok jersey and cap that blacks used to see as a symbol of apartheid, he presented the Rugby World Cup to the victorious South African captain, Francois Pienaar. The sixty-two thousand overwhelmingly Afrikaner spectators, tears streaming, saluted "our president". This crucial episode is brilliantly captured in Clint Eastwood's 2010 film *Invictus*. And, as John Carlin chronicles in *Playing the Enemy*, watching on television a weeping Kobie Coetsee, the police minister who had first broken the ice with Mandela in prison, realised that everything he had tried ten years before had been worth it: '*It was the moment my people, his adversaries, embraced Mandela. This endorses the miracle*'.

In 1996, when Mandela addressed both houses of the British Parliament in its medieval Westminster Hall, the former Conservative prime minister Margaret Thatcher bustled her way to a good seat. '*The ANC is a typical terrorist organization. . . . Anyone who thinks it is going to run the government in South Africa is living in cloud-cuckoo land*', she had said just ten years before, specifically denouncing Mandela as a "terrorist". But like all his other former opponents, he forgave her too.

Even one of his flaws turned out to be of benefit, according to his close comrade and early mentor, Walter Sisulu, who said that, although Mandela had a tendency to trust people too readily—to take people too easily at face value—'*perhaps it is not a failing . . . because the truth is that he has not let us down on account of that confidence he has in people*'. In other words, that flaw became an attribute because it enabled him to reach out to his old enemies, in search of some goodness.

As his physical health deteriorated, he vigorously supported causes across the globe in the twenty-first century: peace negotiations in Burundi and the campaign to make world poverty history. He would speak at a rally in London or travel to an African peace summit in rural Tanzania. Even in his mid-eighties, his schedule was punishing until, finally, in June 2004, he announced to the media in his twinkling Madiba way, '*I am retiring from retirement*'.

He was visibly frailer when I met him with a few invited guests over a special breakfast before the unveiling of his statue in Parliament Square, London, in August 2007, and his aides explained that he tired quickly. Nevertheless, he was still wise cracking and relaxed. Later that morning, helped to walk slowly and hesitantly up to the podium, he seemed very old and unsteady.

But then, when it came to his speech, all the power and oratory returned. He recalled standing with Oliver Tambo there during his visit in 1962: '*We half-joked that we hoped that one day a statue of a black person would be erected here. Oliver would have been proud today*', he remarked, tears welling up at the memory of his close comrade, sadly dead.

I have spent all my life dreaming of a golden age in which all problems will be solved and our wildest hopes fulfilled.

His frailty was all too evident in April 2009 when he appeared, seated and without speaking, on a preelection ANC rally alongside the new president to be, his former Robben Island compatriot Jacob Zuma, and on December 4, 2009, when Mandela gave a video message at the official draw for 2010 FIFA World Cup in South Africa. On February 11, 2010, frail, silent, but beaming and waving, ninety-one-year-old Mandela attended the state opening of South Africa's Parliament, deliberately timed to coincide with the twentieth anniversary of his release from prison. Delighted members of Parliament, led by Zuma, cheered and sang, '*Nelson Mandela, there is none like you*'.

Much of Mandela's time had been, and still was after his presidency, fundraising for his charity to combat HIV-AIDS, and he spoke at a huge pop concert beamed internationally from London's Hyde Park to celebrate his ninetieth birthday in 2008 and to support 46664, his charitable Foundation on HIV-AIDS, which was named after his prison number.

His work on HIV-AIDS conspicuously distinguished him from his successor, President Thabo Mbeki, who for many years seemed in denial about the way the lethal virus was decimating millions of black South Africans and many tens of millions of other Africans across the continent.

Mandela, angry at the desperate consequences of Mbeki's policy of refusing treatment by antiretroviral drugs, was caught by his admirable insistence on not appearing a backseat driver to Mbeki, his successor. Nevertheless, he addressed the Thirteenth International AIDS conference in Durban in July 2000, demanding that *'we proceed to address the needs and concerns of those suffering and dying'*. Two months later Mandela stated publicly that HIV definitely caused AIDS, infuriating Mbeki who refused his requests to meet and who was by now seething at *'the old man's meddling'*. Mbeki orchestrated open public attacks on Mandela over AIDS and even arranged for Mandela to be heckled when he was invited to address a special AIDS policy meeting of the ANC's National Executive in March 2002. Maintaining an almost imperious, but as always polite, dignity in the face of unprecedented jeering by Mbeki loyalists, Mandela's strictly private sense of depression at what he felt was a betrayal by his beloved ANC was tempered by his knowledge that most ANC activists were on his side. There was widespread support for Mandela's stance, especially his belief that common humanity demanded that at least the lives of babies of pregnant women who were HIV-positive should be saved by antiretroviral drugs. And he was widely praised for breaking a taboo by publicly announcing in July 2005 that his fifty-four-year-old son, Makgatho, had died of AIDS.

But Mandela was always scrupulous in his refusal directly to criticize the policies of Mbeki's government. Whatever his disagreements, they either remained private or were expressed in a way that made it clear where he stood, not in contradiction to the ANC to which he remained, as he had always been, steadfastly loyal.

However, he remained tormented, not just by the AIDS crisis engulfing his fellow Africans but also by the havoc and terror unleashed by the autocratic Robert Mugabe in adjacent Zimbabwe. Speaking at a United Nations event in Johannesburg in May 2000, Mandela gave vent to his anger with Mugabe, when he referred to those African leaders who *'once commanded liberation*

armies and despise the very people who put them in power and think it's a
privilege to be there for eternity. Everyone knows well who I am talking
about'. At a private meeting in his London hotel in 2002, I raised
Zimbabwe with him. His frustration and anger with Mugabe was
all too evident, and he started to spell it out—then abruptly dismissed the subject, waving his hand: '*Peter, you must speak to my*
president', he said, evidently concerned that he was being tempted
to breach his self-imposed protocol of loyalty to his successor.

In July 2008, with Zimbabwe almost destroyed and Mugabe
clinging onto office despite losing the presidential election, Mandela finally denounced '*the tragic failure of leadership in our neighboring*
Zimbabwe' at a fundraising dinner in London. During his own presidency, Mandela's relations with Mugabe had been poor, the
prickly, preening Mugabe openly resenting a much bigger liberation hero than he himself was, and Mandela disliking Mugabe's rising despotism and self-serving corruption. Famed journalist Allister
Sparks recalled a conversation with Mandela: '*We got to talking about*
Mugabe, whom he really profoundly disliked, and I think it was recipro-
cated. He said: "You know Allister, the trouble with Mugabe is that he
was the star—and then the sun came up".'

—

And this was Mandela's other strong characteristic. He was invariably a pinnacle of diplomacy and courtesy. But he also tended to
say and do what he thought was right. So he visited Cuba and
praised its many achievements, despite the ire it provoked among
his otherwise good friends in Washington and London. He did so
because he admired the way Cubans had created excellent health
and other public services despite blanket American sanctions, and
above all because Cuban soldiers had fought and died against South
African forces during the grim apartheid days; he was always loyal
to those who had supported his own long walk to freedom and that
of his people.

His close relationship with London and Washington was also
put under strain by his outspoken condemnation of the 2003 invasion of Iraq. '*A big mistake, Peter. A very big mistake. It is wrong. Why*

has Tony done this after all his support for Africa?' he asked me as a member of Prime Minister Blair's cabinet: '*This will cause huge damage internationally'*. I had never heard him speak so angrily—but, as history showed, he was proved correct. The Iraq invasion and its aftermath was indeed a disaster.

It was very far from the vision of global relations he developed on Robben Island, as indeed were the inevitable problems of the new rainbow democracy that was his proudest achievement. The South Africa he bequeathed, joyously liberated from its apartheid nightmare, was seen as an example to the entire world. But overcoming the legacy of apartheid and achieving a more equal society inevitably took much, much longer than many South Africans, as well as the rest of the world, had expected. The staggering crime rate (that also affected whites, whereas under apartheid it took place primarily in the black townships) seemed insoluble. The deliberate apartheid policy of ensuring that black South Africans were prevented from acquiring the education necessary to play their part in the workforce of a modern industrialized society left three-quarters of the population lacking necessary skills, with black unemployment nearly 40 percent, and unlikely to be substantially reduced until the new young black generation has obtained those skills.

Perhaps the most intriguing question about Mandela is, what if he had come to power much earlier, perhaps when other countries in Africa started enjoying democratic, one-person one-vote elections in the early 1960s? Would he have been such a good president? He would have been a much younger and more dynamic president had he come to office in his mid-forties rather than his mid-seventies. But whether he would have been a good president is another matter. Prison gave him wisdom and matured his sense of humanity, except perhaps for the corrosive impact on his inability to be a father and husband. It made him altogether a better leader, principled and tough, yes, but less confrontational and much more consensual, with not an ounce of arrogance, able to wow the world and at home inspire both blacks and reassure worried whites. I am not sure those whites would have given up power for anybody else.

⁓

By the time he attended the World Cup Final at Soccer City stadium in Johannesburg in July 2010, Mandela's deteriorating health was abundantly evident as he arrived wrapped in thick coat and Russian-type fur hat to brave the winter cold, enthusiastically but unavoidably supported by his wife Graça Machel.

Nevertheless, his iconic charisma still radiated. Beaming and waving, nearly 85,000 spectators gave him a thunderous standing ovation, with roars, applause and deafening blasts on their "vuvuzelas", the raucous trumpet-like blowing horns which had been the hallmark of the matches during the finals.

Mandela graced the biggest sporting event in Africa's history—one that would not have been secured in the first placed without his active advocacy. He had '*passed a late fitness test to make the final*' somebody tweeted.

But the next few years were to prove the toughest of his life. '*I never want to grow old*', his indefatigable and ultra-loyal personal assistant Zelda la Grange sadly told me on a visit to London. She discreetly explained his predicament, confined to his Johannesburg home with special medical-support apparatus.

Meanwhile there were squalid squabbles among his close descendants, some seemingly more anxious to bask in his reflected glory and claim his heritage than maintain family dignity around this most dignified, magnanimous and proud of statesmen.

At times it seemed as if he could trust only his devoted aides at the Nelson Mandela Foundation, including of course Zelda, with each of whom he interacted and received support from on a daily basis. He continued to come into the Foundation's centre in Houghton almost daily and work in his personal office there until, unable to continue, he was helped to walk slowly out in November 2010, leaving a profound emptiness. The office still remains as he left it for the last time that day, so that invited visitors can witness, pause and imagine him at work there.

But as the end beckoned even the Foundation's staff closest to him were kept at a distance, frustrated that they could not protect him in the way they had always done, just as he was becoming so vulnerable.

Meanwhile he had loved having more time to spend with his children, grand-children and great-grandchildren. His daughter Zindzi described how the little ones kept him grounded, taking him with them into the garden, teasing, even scolding him. She added: '*My father is a very loving person, but he still finds it hard to be physical because he had no physical contact for so many years*'.

In *Long Walk to Freedom* Mandela had written of Zindzi: '*I am sure it was not easy for her finally to see a father she had never known, a father who could love her only at a distance, who seemed to belong not to her but to the people*'. In turn, she explained how she had realised after he walked out of prison '*that as much as I wanted my father to come back home to me, he was coming back to the nation*'.

Zindzi had been four months old when he went on the run, and a year-and-a-half old when he was arrested, then sentenced to life imprisonment. '*For a long time after his release there was a lot of bitterness*', she explained. '*I never ever imagined my father being president. I imagined him coming him and having a normal family life. When he come out of prison we only had a few moments with him as a family, before the reception committee joined us. I realised then "he's still not mine".*'

Near the end of April 2013 the 94-year-old received a visit from President Zuma and other senior ANC officials, a television camera in tow. Three weeks had passed since his release after a ten-day stay in hospital, the third time in five months that he had been hospitalized for a lung infection. The South African Broadcast Corporation video showed him in an armchair, head propped up on a pillow, legs on a footrest with a blanket over him. Journalists considered what appeared to be marks on his face were from a recently removed oxygen mask.

Zuma joked with his ANC colleagues, family members and the medical team. But Mandela remained determinedly unresponsive, ashen, rigidly unsmiling and staring straight ahead. At one point Zuma tried to hold Mandela's hand evidently without response, so covered it with his own. It was an excruciatingly awkward encounter, done it seemed for the publicity rather than according to Mandela's wishes, as his close aide subsequently confirmed. '*He was furious*', one told me.

From 1990, after he had emerged from prison, everyone wanted a piece of Mandela, some genuine, others decidedly not. A close and trusted comrade of his once told me: '*Madiba brings out the worst in everyone*'.

That certainly appeared to be true of a book published by Penguin Random House in mid-2017 and then withdrawn after fierce complaints led by his widow Graça Machel. *Mandela's Last Years* was authored by physician Vejay Ramlakan, the manager of his medical team, depicted as his personal doctor.

The Nelson Mandela Foundation, always a ready helper for authors and researchers, was not consulted and issued a coruscating statement. The book '*demonstrates both ignorance and prejudice*' and is full of '*inaccuracies, falsehoods and invasions of privacy*', the NMF stated. '*It's "hallmark", in our view, is a pattern of disclosure which uses the privilege of private space to discredit certain people and promote others. So that, fundamentally, this is not a book about Madiba but rather about the author's cast of "good guys" and "bad guys"*.'

Although nobody in the know seemed to doubt the authenticity, accuracy and completeness of the medical data Ramlakan shared, they did question the ethics of the disclosures. The NMF concluded: '*It is not an easy thing for us to support the withdrawal of a book. We oppose censorship in principle and work hard at avoiding the role of gatekeeper. Madiba repeatedly communicated to us an imperative not to be tripped up by a desire to protect him. Always, however, there are limits. And* Mandela's Last Years *is beyond them*'.

However, the book did confirm what many informed people

speculated: that President Zuma did everything needed to keep Mandela alive for as long as possible—no matter what the price to his dignity or to the public purse.

The author constantly marshaled evidence to support his claim that Mandela was crystal clear until the end. Yet from his ninetieth birthday in 2008 onward, those closest to Mandela saw the fading of his mental powers. Towards the end of his life some, like his old legal friend George Bizos, spoke about it, although there was an admirable wish to demonstrate some sensitivity and confidentiality by those closest to him. Why, they asked, did the author promote this myth? Whose interests did it serve? And why was it so partially positive to some, notably President Zuma, and always negative to others? It seemed to Zuma critics more than a coincidence that the book appeared at a time when the British-based global public affairs company, Bell Pottinger, was forced to admit to running a malevolent £1 million campaign of fake news and lies to conceal corruption by the Zuma family and its close business associates, the Gupta brothers. Bell Pottinger went bankrupt as a consequence.

Mandela's steadfast, trusted Robben Island comrade Ahmed Kathrada emotionally described his last visit in hospital: '*I was filled with an overwhelming mixture of sadness, emotion and pride. He tightly held my hand until the end of my brief visit. It was profoundly heart-breaking. It brought me to the verge of tears when my thoughts automatically flashed back to the picture of the man I grew up under. How I wished I'd never had to confront the reality of what I saw . . . a giant of a man reduced to a shadow of his former self*'.

After an official announcement in June 2013 that Mandela was in a critical condition, his 95th birthday on 18 July was celebrated by the whole country. At schools children sang "*Happy birthday, Tata Madiba*" and crowds gathered outside his hospital.

But nearly six months later, his ventilator and other life-support were switched off and he was finally allowed to die peacefully on 5 December 2013 at his Houghton home in Johannesburg.

He had always said that when he died, his first step, if he went to heaven, would be to ask how he could join the nearest ANC branch there.

After lying in state in Pretoria for three days he was buried in a curated garden of aloe plants and rocky outcrops atop a slope at Qunu, near his retirement home in his beloved Transkei, and a little way from his birthplace.

Not just the nation but the whole world mourned the passing of one of the most special and revered figures in human history.

—

Gandhi. Kennedy. Churchill. All iconic figures, the charismatic first two the more so for being assassinated, the last for his inspirational wartime leadership. Yet ask almost anybody, anywhere, which global statesman they admire most and "Nelson Mandela" will likely as not be the answer. Other world figures are usually famous within their own professional disciplines, sections of society, interest groups or age groups. Many attract hostility, cynicism or plain indifference. Mandela's unique achievement was to command fame, admiration and affection from virtually everyone, everywhere in the world.

So, if he is more iconic than anybody else—then, why?

His life story of sacrifice, courage, endurance and suffering, in the great and noble cause of liberty, democracy and justice, places him among a very select few: Chartists, suffragettes, Gandhi himself, anticolonial African leaders, Che Guevara, Lech Walesa and Aleksandr Solzhenitsyn, to name just some.

But Mandela towers above them all in popular imagination. Perhaps in part this is because he is the first such figure to be projected to the world's peoples through the powerful media of modern, global television and the internet. He is quite simply far better known than any comparable figure. But equally, he survived and indeed prospered, even under the fierce media spotlight of twenty-four-hour news, overhype and journalistic spin, where (uniquely) he remained untarnished and undiminished, despite that modern media beast's unsurpassed capacity for building up and then knocking down, leaving Mandela serenely above all its insatiable prurience and obsession for triviality and instant novelty. Where most political careers end in failure or opprobrium, Mandela's continued to soar, long after he had stepped down as president.

Mandela's greatness, his stature, derives not just from an extraordinary biography that dwarfed the rest of humankind. It also comes from the humanity that he radiated, his common touch, humility, self-deprecation, sense of fun and dignity. Prison could have embittered, adulation could have gone to his head and egotism could have triumphed. The clutching of the crowd and the intrusive pressures of the modern political age could have seen him retreat behind the barriers that most top figures today erect around them simply to retain some individual space but that all too often end up either in cold aloofness or in patent insincerity and its companion cynicism. But none of this happened. Throughout everything, Nelson Mandela remained his own man, not seduced by the trappings of office or deluded by the adulation of admirers, always friendly and approachable. And that is why he is the icon of icons—and maybe always will be.

A leader must also tend his garden; he, too, sows seeds and then watches, cultivates and harvests the result. Like the gardener, a leader must take responsibility for what he cultivates; he must mind his work, try to repel enemies, preserve what can be preserved, and eliminate what cannot succeed.

· *10* ·

Legacy Betrayed?

*M*andela's extraordinary leadership and insistence on reconciliation transformed South Africa from a police state into a constitutional democracy. After a relatively peaceful and smooth process, the country emerged from behind its ugly white veil to proudly take its rightful place as a leading—perhaps *the* leading—African state.

The main African-led organisations in the freedom struggle had always promoted the idea of an inclusive South Africa, and the subsequent achievements of the ANC government were considerable. Not just under President Mandela, but also his successors, Thabo Mbeki and Jacob Zuma. Achievements even more remarkable given the horrendous legacy of apartheid: the sprawling shanty towns; the lack of health care; the forced displacements; and the dehumanising education system, designed to keep the black majority as servants for white masters.

The challenge for the new democracy was how to create a prosperous, united, rights-based society when 80 percent of people lived in endemic poverty. From the time Mandela took office in 1994, the problem was exacerbated by a growing population. This was further complicated by continuous migration from impoverished rural subsistence economies to harsh urban squatter destitution, and an influx of over two million African immigrants from countries as diverse and distant as Somalia and Zimbabwe. Consequently, the demand on government for basic services seemed insatiable: as fast as new houses were built, new shacks appeared beside them.

Yet in its first twenty years of democratic government, the ANC built more than three million new homes and created four million jobs. Millions more South Africans secured running water and electricity. Some economists say that income per capita, in real terms, rose by almost a third. Importantly the ANC created a welfare state, providing a vital safety net of social security payments: a lifeline for up to 17 million people, from the elderly to the unemployed, constituting a third of the population. In addition, substantial state bursaries opened up the country's universities to over 400,000 new students: mostly black. And, as a result of innovative health programmes (particularly those focusing on HIV and TB), life expectancy improved, with child mortality dramatically reduced.

In the new South Africa, the judiciary gained powers envied by most other democracies. The Constitutional Court could (and did) annul statutes of parliament it deemed to contravene the country's Bill of Rights, and it censured President Zuma following serious breaches of his constitutional obligations.

South Africa's well-regulated financial system weathered the international crisis of 2008 better than many and, although about one million jobs were lost over the next couple of years in the global slump, its economy was still reasonably robust. Basic infrastructure compared favourably with so-called developed nations, and was certainly by far the best in Africa. The country's wealthy economy accounted for fully a fifth of Africa's total GDP with just a twentieth of the continent's population: 50 million out of one thousand million.

Ranked high in the United Nation's measure of attractiveness for foreign direct investment, with strong financial institutions, banks, stock market and a good corporate governance and regulatory framework, South Africa was an attractive foreign investor

destination. Market analysts tended to like South African companies and the way that they are led and managed.

In 2011 the country joined Brazil, Russia, India and China in
the powerful BRICS grouping, hailed as the dawn of a new era:
one in which South Africa would become the gateway for economic growth throughout the continent—the Dubai of Africa.

In 2012, it was also high in the World Bank's Ease of Doing
Business Index, ahead of Spain and Italy. But just five years later,
with corruption and cronyism rampant under President Zuma and
a downgrade by global credit agencies to near-junk status, the 2017
Index ranked South Africa just 74th, having fallen well behind
Spain at 32nd and Italy at 50th.

After the great promise of the Mandela years, the transformation to a more equal society inevitably took much, much longer
than most South Africans—and indeed the rest of the world—had
hoped.

High violent crime rates affected whites (unlike under apartheid, when such crime was primarily limited to black townships).
The apartheid policy of preventing black South Africans from
acquiring the necessary education to work in a modern industriali-
sed society adversely affected three quarters of the population.
Black unemployment hovered around 40 percent, and was unlikely
to be much reduced until a younger generation obtained skills,
with youth unemployment as high as 50 percent in some areas.

Although a new black professional class quickly emerged and
prospered, black workers did not benefit as much as they should
have from the country's post-1994 growth and stability. Indeed the
gap between rich and poor in the new South Africa was more pro-
nounced than almost any other country.

⁓

Mandela's ANC inspired the world. But by the time he died (aged
95) in December 2013, the party's leadership at all levels was
betraying the values and integrity he had epitomised.

As early as August 1998 he had warned in a presidential

speech: 'We have learnt now that even those people with whom we fought the struggle against apartheid's corruption can themselves become corrupted.' It proved a prescient warning—though nothing could have prepared him for what was to come.

In his last years, Mandela was deeply pained by a corrosive increase in cronyism and corruption. Reluctant to criticise his successors publicly, he privately felt betrayed and bitterly disappointed. He realised that many of his former comrades, led by Zuma, had abandoned his legacy, causing deep disillusion among his people, and sparking widespread local 'service delivery' protests and strikes on a daily basis.

Nowhere was this clearer than in schooling. Although the ANC government spent more on education than any other developing nation, and managed to double black school attendance from apartheid days, black schools found themselves very short of textbooks—not because there were insufficient funds, but because budgets were badly managed or siphoned off through dodgy tender processes.

Protected by ANC leaders in return for political support, the powerful South African Democratic Teachers Union (SADTU) seemed to have forgotten its proud history in the freedom struggle. In 2015, the weekly *City Press* newspaper exposed a jobs-for-cash racket, run by teacher-union officials. Frequently SADTU protected bad or lazy teachers. Subsequent investigations revealed that the union was also running a 'complex patronage system' in several provincial education departments.

No wonder that school standards suffered.

Out of 140 countries in the World Economic Forum's Global Competitiveness Index (2015–2016), South Africa was ranked at 138 for the quality of its education, below desperately poor, undeveloped states like Burundi, Benin and Mauritania: an appalling, almost criminal indictment of Mandela's successors.

But in spite of this dire predicament, the hunger for education remained unabated, especially in the most poverty-stricken areas of the country. Every year, inspiring stories emerged of students overcoming incredible odds to pass their exams, often studying by candlelight on an empty stomach.

I have met teachers in predominantly black residential areas who take great pride in high standards—only to despair when their bright, well-qualified pupils fail to find jobs. One such pupil ended up as a gardener at his old school in Pretoria, where once he had excelled academically. Sadly, he is one of the lucky ones. Unemployment among black youth has remained shockingly high.

The extent to which corruption had spread like a disease throughout society was confirmed in December 2017, when Public Protector Busi Mkhwebane found that monies intended for Mandela's 2013 funeral had been stolen by Eastern Cape government officials. The Nelson Mandela Foundation reacted with 'outrage' at this theft of public funds, and called for 'definitive action against those who were fingered' in the Public Protector's report.

Corruption and cronyism quickly began to ruin the economy. During the presidencies of Nelson Mandela and Thabo Mbeki, government debt was reduced from the high apartheid level of 52 percent of GDP to less than 30 percent. But under Jacob Zuma it jumped sharply to over 46 percent and stayed upon an upward trajectory. GDP per capita declined annually; unemployment rose further from terrifying levels; and fixed investment all but collapsed. Productivity remained poor and falling while most competitor countries' rates shot up.

As the country's credit rating was downgraded again in late 2017, Bonang Mohale, chief executive officer of Business Leadership South Africa, which represents about 80 of the country's biggest companies, said: 'Many economic and political problems South Africans experience are rooted in corruption, state capture and political patronage resulting in a trust deficit,' adding that business and investor confidence in South Africa was at a 30-year low.

A remorseless policy of 'state capture' had systematically propped up and enriched a criminal power elite at the expense of the country. Extraordinary influence and power was ceded by President Zuma to his close business associates the Indian-South Africa

Gupta brothers. State Owned Enterprises such as South African Airways and the country's electricity generator Eskom were shamelessly looted—vividly shown through evidence given in a public inquiry conducted by a Committee of the South African Parliament in 2017.

For instance Eskom virtually 'gave' billions to the Gupta/ Zuma syndicate, through contrived 'consulting' contracts, tenders for fictitious goods and services, and advances to allow them to buy the coal mines from which they then sold back over-priced, poor quality coal. With incompetent and shady 'Zupta' cronies appointed to run both SAA and Eskom, they were plunged into debt, and had to be rescued by multibillion taxpayer bailouts.

The extent of mismanagement and productivity meltdown was revealed in late 2017 by investment analyst Andrew Lapping. Eskom's electricity production was the same as in 2003, he pointed out. Yet it employed 50 percent more people and paid them almost double the real wages of 14 years previously, to deliver the same amount of power. No mystery that tax payers had to keep coughing up billions in bailouts.

In the late 1990s, the radiance of Nelson Mandela's 'rainbow nation' shone down upon the world, consigning apartheid to history. But two decades later, South Africa had fallen from hero to zero. With a political leadership and its business crony elite looting the country, international investors turned their backs on a nation they once favoured, and—generations ago—colonially plundered.

Yet, through all this, debates over the country's future often seemed parochial. Of course serious economic transformation remained essential to reduce and ideally eliminate the still grossly unequal distribution of wealth and land between white and black. And of course it should not have been pursued in a way that was tantamount to taxpayer theft, as occurred under the Zuma presidency. But many South Africans have conducted the debate over economic transformation as if the country was insulated from intense global competition.

For example, every year there are 7.5 million new Chinese

graduates and 7 million new Indian graduates, mostly in science, engineering, technology and ICT. By contrast South Africa produces 180,000 new graduates. Of course it is a much smaller country, but proportionately South Africa produces only *half* their annual graduate numbers.

Thus, South Africa is being undercut: on low cost, high skills and quality not just by these two economic superpowers but by many other countries. The only way to prosper in today's globalised world is through high skills and investment, but South Africa is dangerously lacking on both counts. This is especially worrying in light of the new technological revolution of robotics and Artificial Intelligence, as some experts from advanced economies suggest two-thirds of primary school children will grow up to do jobs which have not yet been invented.

—

The date 16 August 2012 should forever be etched in South Africa's collective memory.

In scenes eerily reminiscent of the country's apartheid years, the police opened fire on striking black mineworkers at Lonmin's Marikana platinum mine near Rustenburg, west of Johannesburg. Thirty-four people died, and 78 were injured. Shockingly, at least 14 of the dead were hunted down and shot from behind, some distance from the main protest area.

Lawyers representing families of the dead miners insisted that the massacre was pre-planned by senior figures in the police and in the Zuma government, invoking chilling testimony that 'weapons of war' were used instead of proper riot control procedures. Guns were planted on some of the corpses, and witnesses claimed to have been intimidated—even tortured—by the predominantly black police.

The Marikana massacre seemed to symbolise the unresolved legacy of apartheid: a wealthy white-owned corporation pitted against its poor, black migrant workers. Most of them lived in the shadow of the mine at Wonderkop: a sprawling 'informal' settlement of 40,000 people, with no running water, no proper electricity, no sewage or sanitation.

In December 2012, seven hundred miles to the south, close to Mandela's birthplace in rural, remote Transkei, I met the widow of one of the murdered strikers. She carried a small baby on her back. Her situation was desperate because the family's meagre income had suddenly been destroyed. Despite the ANC-established welfare system, it was hard to see how two decades of democracy had made any improvement to the living standards of the rural poor like her.

Under apartheid, government and big business were run exclusively by the white minority. When white rule finally came to an end, the fear was that white businesses and investors would flee.

Instead under Mandela's guidance, a deal was struck, and compromises were made for the sake of a peaceful and economically stable transition. Thus, a black majority now ran the government but the white minority still ran the economy.

In retrospect it is hard to see how any other course could have been adopted by Mandela and the ANC leadership. More radical change at the time would undoubtedly have triggered a flight of capital, financial calamity and political turmoil. There would also have been a real risk of national rather than partial civil war, and Mozambique and Angola—societies torn apart and plagued by landmines, infrastructure destruction and economic chaos—are salutary examples of the consequences of non-negotiated transformations. But some, like former ANC liberation hero and subsequent ANC Minister Ronnie Kasrils, subsequently saw this as 'the devil's pact': a terrible betrayal of the poorest of the poor.

It should be acknowledged that companies like Lonmin did bring black South Africans into their senior management. A new black business elite was empowered—even creating some billionaires—and South Africa gained a sizeable new black middle class, including state bureaucrats, ANC politicians and ANC-linked trade union leaders affiliated to the Confederation of South African Trade Unions (COSATU). But the fundamental divide bequeathed by apartheid remained, and the inequality gap grew.

The ideological trajectory combined with chronically bad political leadership had dire consequences for post-1994 South Africa. Surely the priority now is to develop a new social compact, where privilege and reward are renegotiated in favour of a more equal dispensation in which wealth and economic power are sacrificed by the few and shared with the many?

The alternative could be a revolution of rising expectations and frustration, in which South Africa could once again become as ungovernable as it was during the darkest years of apartheid.

By 2010, Zwelinzima Vavi, the former Secretary General of COSATU and one time ally of President Zuma, was already warning: 'We're headed for a predator state, where a powerful, corrupt and demagogic elite of political hyenas is increasingly using the state to get rich.'

Prophetic words indeed.

—

Mandela always championed freedom of expression.

He once declared: 'None of our irritations with the perceived inadequacies of the media should ever allow us to suggest that the independence of the press should be compromised or coerced. A bad free press is preferable to a technically good, subservient press.'

However, Zuma's attitude to the media was radically different. In 2013, Parliament passed his Protection of State Information Bill, known colloquially as the 'Secrecy Bill'. It invoked draconian powers to prevent journalists from exposing corruption, nepotism and state abuse.

In the preceding five years, media practitioners and civil society activists had managed to force several significant moderating amendments—further evidence of the resilience of South Africa's democratic culture. But the Bill was still passed by a weak parliament dominated by an ANC faction that remained almost entirely loyal to President Zuma to the bitter end.

Yet, Zuma did not sign the Bill into law. Perhaps he was aware that, if his government attempted to use the legislation to crack down on freedom of expression, several civil society organisations were on stand-by, determined to take the case to the Constitutional Court and confident of a positive ruling. The strength of South Africa's rule of law remained a bulwark against undemocratic conduct.

True, the erosion of Mandela's legacy continued. But there were also countervailing pressures from within his ANC—and crucially, vocal non-governmental organisations and law centres such as the Council for the Advancement of the South African Constitution (CASAC) and Section 27—which were ready and willing to use the rights enshrined in the Constitution to hold to account those in power. Moreover, the independent Constitutional Court delivered damaging judgements against President Zuma, while former Public Protector, the indomitable advocate Thuli Madonsela, spotlighted corrupt dealings including serious transgressions committed by the president.

Inevitably, increasing government corruption (master-minded by Jacob Zuma and his network of cronies, like the infamous Guptas) encouraged 'jaundiced whites' to become more vocal. Such people had reluctantly praised the 'Mandela miracle', but never accepted the consequences: namely that their grotesquely privileged existence had to go. As the Zuma presidency became mired in scandal, they barely concealed their smirks, proclaiming 'I told you so', but conveniently forgetting their complicity in apartheid, and the affluence they had enjoyed at the expense of mass misery.

The perpetuation of shady practice in the traditionally white business sector was also dramatically revealed towards the end of 2017, when Steinhoff International imploded.

It was South Africa's seventh largest company by market

value, and it finally admitted to having massaged its financial statements to fuel a debt-driven international acquisition spree. After continuously and aggressively denying allegations of impropriety, the company belatedly confessed when auditors Deloitte refused to sign off on the accounts for the year to end September 2017. With its CEO Markus Jooste resigning in disgrace, Steinhoff's share price dropped more than 90 percent, wiping out over R200 billion in paper wealth, much of it owned by South African investors.

—

Perhaps longstanding ANC supporters like me expected too much of the 'rainbow nation'. Perhaps it was naïve to think that Mandela's ANC—for all its noble history and tradition of moral integrity and constitutionalism—could be immune to human frailty, especially in the face of such immense social inequality and global power imbalances.

Could any political party anywhere (including in rich, old democracies like Britain) have done any better? I served for twelve years in Labour's social democratic British government, and we found it tough to advance social justice whilst delivering economic success in a world gripped by the inequality-increasing, growth-stifling economics of neoliberalism.

The notion of the 'Mandela miracle' was grounded in reality, but it also engendered myth. The transition from brutal apartheid to rainbow democracy encouraged a tendency to frame the South African story too simplistically.

Outside observers have never been able to view post-apartheid South Africa in a nuanced way: they either romanticise or cynically dismiss it. But neither of these perceptions is accurate—and they never were. After the relatively painless transition from apartheid under Mandela, it was always going to be a bumpy road.

The apartheid heritage of democratic South Africa is deeply rooted in massive social inequality and economic division: as well as institutionalised racism. Yet it is judged by Britain, Europe and the US according to far higher standards than they apply to themselves.

It should also be remembered that many ANC members still embody basic decency, dedication and moral principles: in stark contrast to the insidious corruption of the Zuma presidency. And ANC 'stalwarts', like Pravin Gordhan (perhaps the most courageously prominent), struggled to keep Mandela's legacy alive.

In policy terms too, the party remained largely true to Mandela's original values, as exemplified by the National Development Plan 2030 that was developed under the leadership of Cyril Ramaphosa and former finance minister, Trevor Manuel. Indeed, the ANC's programme presents a credible alternative to the global grip of neoliberalism for those seeking a social democratic agenda in a market economy.

In December 2017, Mandela's widow Graça Machel said that South Africans should stop agonising about how the country Mandela created had 'slipped through their hands'. Instead, they should remember his famous words: 'It is in your hands to make of the world a better place for all.'

South Africa was 'an extraordinary country', Machel said. A singular country in which a singular generation—that of Mandela, Albert Luthuli, Oliver Tambo, Walter Sisulu, Ahmed Kathrada, Beyers Naude, Winnie Madikizela-Mandela, and Helen Joseph amongst others—had led their compatriots to freedom. And that, Machel added, could be repeated: 'If this country, a century back, could produce such leaders it has to be able to produce another crop. It is in South Africa's genes, in its DNA.'

Perhaps the 'Born Frees'—those young South Africans who never knew formal apartheid, and who comprise over 40 percent of the population—will reclaim Mandela's legacy for the twenty-first century. They have certainly flexed their muscles on university campuses in the last couple of years, showing an eagerness to engage with politics, at times with a militancy that shook the complacency of some of those institutions.

—

South Africa is a beautiful country which remains an inspiration: marvellous to visit, and joyously transformed from the evil days of apartheid when I left as a teenager in 1966. And, despite all that has betrayed his legacy, Mandela bequeathed a series of crucial, powerful countervailing forces to elitism, inequality and corruption.

First, a vigorous political opposition that has made advances especially at city and municipal government level.

Second, a vibrant civil society, forged originally during the anti-apartheid struggle, and resurrected both to challenge any attempt by the ruling ANC to undermine democratic structures and processes, and to demand a renewed leadership in harmony with the Mandela vision.

Third, a vigorously independent media: outspoken talk radio stations; respected and fearlessly investigative online publications such as *Daily Maverick* and *BizNews*; and good newspapers like *Business Day*, *Mail & Guardian* and *City Press*.

Fourth, the South African judiciary has powers envied by most other democracies; and the Constitutional Court can (and *does*) annul statutes of parliament which are deemed to contravene the country's Bill of Rights and has not been shy to rule against the president. The country can be very proud of—and grateful for— the strength of its rule of law and the independence of its judiciary.

Fifth, the country has a solid framework of law, financial regulation, and corporate governance, with a relatively wealthy and resilient economy. There is great business entrepreneurialism at the top—though a deeper entrepreneurial culture needs actively to be supported and promoted in the less formal parts of the economy. But the question for corporate leaders is whether they will actively join the struggle, not just against corruption (from which some have benefitted) but also to encourage fundamental economic transformation. It is not possible credibly to do the first without also doing the second.

Sixth, large numbers of public servants still work hard, resist corruption and political manipulation, and strive for excellence:

although there may not be enough of them, they provide a platform for a new political leadership to build upon.

Indeed, South Africa seemed to have been given a 'get out of jail free card' in December 2017. Cyril Ramaphosa, hugely able, a former struggle stalwart, trade union leader, respected chief negotiator under Mandela, then successful businessman and deputy president, won the presidency of the ANC narrowly with a majority of just 179 votes (2,440 against 2,261). He beat President Zuma's favoured successor, his former wife Nkosazana Dlamini-Zuma. That he won at all was a tribute to his stature, to the fact that trade unions and the SA Communist Party backed him but above all because of huge and vocal civil society demands for change. One very senior ANC figure told me afterwards that the Party would have decisively lost the following election had Ramaphosa been defeated.

Many were astounded that Zuma's formidable party machine had been overcome—not least because it included bribing voting delegates (the going rate for an ANC Branch secretary said to be R50,000, the source speculated to be Russians behind a multi-billion Rand nuclear power deal from which Zuma was due a cut). But, coupled with the election of a substantial cadre of Zuma loyalists elsewhere in the Party leadership, this meant the ANC had released itself from the corrupt Zuma grip and simultaneously remained in entangled within it.

Zuma was left facing 783 charges of corruption and racketeering, with far too many prominent ANC members dependent upon feeding from the state's trough, protected by creeping authoritarianism and state capture. Some critics went so far as to describe the 'criminalisation of the ANC', labelling it a 'patronage machine'. In his 2017 bestselling book, *The President's Keepers* (which the Zuma apparatus sought to suppress), investigative journalist Jacques Pauw described what he called a 'shadow mafia state'. Under Zuma's rule, he wrote 'South Africa has become a two-government country. There is an elected government, and there is a shadow government—a state within a state.'

Despite this, in February 2018—though only under a final ultimatum of an ANC-called Parliamentary no-confidence vote—Zuma eventually and very obviously reluctantly resigned. To the country's enormous relief, Ramaphosa was elected South African President.

Immediately Ramaphosa pledged to be guided by Mandela's example of 'ethical behaviour and ethical leadership'. By vowing to restore good governance in the Mandela tradition, he insisted 'we are not merely honouring the past, we are building the future. We are continuing the long walk he began, to build a society in which all may be free, in which all may be equal before the law and in which all may share in the wealth of our land and have a better life'.

He pledged to fight corruption 'with the same intensity and purpose that we fight poverty, unemployment and inequality' and 'to restore the integrity of the ANC', as well to as root out cronyism and sleaze throughout the public and private sectors. His was an ambitious programme and the very future of the country rested on Ramaphosa's ability to carry it through.

After a terribly debilitating interlude, 'Mandela's rainbow nation was being reborn' many said or desperately hoped—though the challenges remained daunting.

—

Mandela was no saint—for example his activism was at the expense of his family relationships, and as a young man he was something of a lothario with a well-developed sense of his own self-importance. Also, his government, anxious to achieve a smooth transition and encourage international investment after efforts to prop up apartheid in its dying years had virtually bankrupted the country, rather too readily embraced elements of the neoliberal global economic order—something criticised by a younger generation questioning his legacy.

But Mandela's towering stature and vision will nevertheless

remain the yardstick by which South Africa's future will be measured, and his successors inevitably judged. He gave the ANC, South Africa and the world a moral compass.

The South African commentator Jonny Steinberg has noted that the country shares many of the features of a post-Trump, Brexit world of rapacious inequality in which there is widespread cynicism amongst citizens about the social order and the power of 'opaque corporations'. He predicts that 'we are entering a time in which people's views are becoming wildly unstable, with deep cynicism and blind hope entwined.'

Sadly there will never be another quite like Nelson Mandela, with his courage, humanity and sacrifice, and his commitment to the enduring values of liberty, democracy, integrity, equality and justice.

When Bill Clinton asked him—standing in his old Robben Island cell—how Mandela could bear no resentment against his jailers, he answered very simply: 'if I had succumbed to revenge I would never have been able to achieve what I did.'

A generation of South Africans sacrificed their lives to overcome apartheid and generate the Mandela legacy. Tens of thousands suffered imprisonment, torture and exile in the process, my brave parents I'm proud to say amongst them. South Africa will not succeed unless the spirit and principles of the Mandela years are reclaimed.

One of his many memorable proverbs stands as a beacon for all humankind as we face up to serious new threats and challenges—from climate change and terrorism, to Artificial Intelligence and inequality:

What counts in life is not the mere fact that we have lived. It is what difference we have made to the lives of others.

Selected Bibliography

Benson, Mary. *Nelson Mandela: The Man and the Movement*. London: Penguin, 1994.

Carlin, John. *Playing the Enemy*. London: Grove Atlantic, 2008.

Hain, Peter. *Sing the Beloved Country: The Struggle for the New South Africa*. London: Pluto, 1996.

la Grange, Zelda. *Good Morning, Mr. Mandela*. London: Penguin, 2014.

Mandela, Nelson. *Long Walk to Freedom*. London: Little, Brown, 1994.

Mandela, Nelson, with Mandla Langa. *Dare Not Linger: The Presidential Years*. London: Macmillan, 2017.

Mandela, Winnie. *Part of My Soul*. Edited by Anne Benjamin and adapted by Mary Benson. London: Penguin, 1985.

Mandela: The Authorised Portrait. London: Bloomsbury, 2006.

Meredith, Martin. *Nelson Mandela*. London: Hamish Hamilton, 1997.

Reader, John. *Africa: A Biography of the Continent*. London: Penguin, 1998.

Sampson, Anthony. *Mandela*. London: HarperCollins, 1999.

Troup, Freda. *South Africa: An Historical Introduction*. London: Penguin, 1975.

Index

About the Author

Peter Hain is well known for a lifetime of anti-apartheid campaigning. Born to anti-apartheid activists with links to Mandela going back to the 1950s, he grew up in South Africa where his parents were jailed, then banned and finally exiled to Britain by the regime. The effectiveness of Hain's fervent campaigning in the 1970s made him a target of the regime's security services.

Subsequently a Labour MP and government minister, Peter Hain served in several prominent Cabinet positions including Secretary of State for Northern Ireland, Secretary of State for Work and Pensions, and Leader of the House of Commons. He is now a member of the House of Lords and Visiting Professor at Wits Business School, Johannesburg. A regular contributor to the daily nationals, he is also the author of twenty books including *Don't Play with Apartheid, Mistaken Identity, A Putney Plot?, Back to the Future of Socialism* and his memoir *Outside In.*